Bonsai

Bonsai

The art of not killing your first tree – A guide for beginners

Clive Woods

Margaret Fisher

KLG Publishing

CONTENTS

Introduction — 1

1 | Chapter 1: History & Tradition — 4

2 | Chapter 2: Benefits & Amazing Facts — 8

3 | Chapter 3: Types of Bonsai — 19

4 | Chapter 4: Getting Started — 22

5 | Chapter 5: Tools & Equipment — 30

6 | Chapter 6: Planting & Soiling — 38

7 | Chapter 7: Fertilizing & Watering — 42

8 | Chapter 8: Styling, Shaping, Wiring & Pruning — 47

9 | Chapter 9: Repotting & Deadwood — 58

10 | Chapter 10: Pests, Disease & Seasonal Maintenance — 62

11 | Chapter 11: Misconceptions & Common Mistakes — 69

CONTENTS

12 | Chapter 12: Profiles of Bonsai Species 83

13 | Chapter 13: Presentation & Display 105

14 | Chapter 14: FAQs 108

15 | Conclusion 121

16 | Resources & Bibliography 123

Copyright © 2022 by Clive Woods

Disclaimer: *The information in this book is not intended as a substitute for professional medical advice, nutritional advice, or financial advice. The author of this book has used their best efforts in the preparation of this book. They make no representation or warranties with respect to the accuracy, applicability, fitness, or completeness of the contents of this book.*
The information contained in this book is strictly for educational purposes. Therefore, if you wish to apply the ideas contained in this book, you are taking full responsibility for your actions. This includes, but is not limited to: information regarding growing and looking after bonsai trees. While many people have successfully grown bonsai trees, past performance may not be indicative of future results. Therefore, no person should assume that the future performance of any gardening or other endeavor will be equal to past performance levels.

First Printing, 2022

Introduction

What was your reaction or feeling the first time you saw a bonsai tree in real life? If you're anything like most people, the experience was probably awe-inspiring—if not confusing! How can such a tiny tree exist that so perfectly replicates a wild full-size tree growing in nature? How can someone take such meticulous care of a living being that—due to its size—must be so delicate and sensitive? Or how can a living tree survive in such a shallow pot?

For whatever unexpected or inspirational reason, you have been drawn toward the art of bonsai trees at this point in your life. Perhaps it's something you've always considered, but—for whatever reason—you never took the first crucial step. Perhaps you've tried to grow a bonsai tree in the past and felt embarrassed or frustrated when your tree failed to survive or when it failed to manifest into the beautiful shape you hoped for. Maybe you're drawn to bonsai trees for their aesthetics, or to create a living legacy to pass down to the next generation, or even to broaden an existing horticultural skillset. Alternatively, you've tried to learn about growing and caring for bonsai trees online but became frustrated and disheartened with the mess of information assorted across various articles and blog posts. While there is undoubtedly plenty of valuable information online about bonsai trees available, sifting through diverging opinions and trying to make logical sense of all that information is no easy task.

No matter your reason—and what led you to this book—you've made the right decision and you should be proud of yourself for moving in the right direction. This book will give you all the information, skills, tips, and advice you need to grow your own beautiful bonsai trees. It will answer all the questions and concerns you may have—even those that haven't come up yet!

My intention in writing this book is to save you from going down the Google rabbit hole. With this book, you can go from a complete beginner to a knowledgeable bonsai grower by following a sequence of easy-to-understand and practical steps. Now, all you need to do is follow this book from chapter to chapter as presented to you. This includes all the facts, information, procedures, and how-to's that you need to cultivate your first bonsai tree and beyond! Most importantly, by following the advice in this book, you can sidestep the many common disappointments that most beginner bonsai growers meet—killing their first tree (or, more often, their first, second, and third trees!).

This book covers every aspect; from the benefits of growing bonsai and its cultural and historical significance to the various types of trees, how to get started, where to obtain your first tree, the tools, and the equipment that you will need (as well as how much you should expect to pay). Moreover, you'll learn all the practical skills needed to prevent your bonsai from dying, including planting, soiling, fertilizing, watering, styling, shaping, pruning, repotting, and creating deadwood.

Next, we'll take a detailed look at troubleshooting the various issues that can affect your trees, including pests, diseases, and seasonal considerations. Bonsai tree troubleshooting continues with an in-depth look at the common mistakes new bonsai growers make that, unfortunately, kill their trees, and insights on how you can avoid these pitfalls. The book then concludes with a detailed FAQs section, where other questions or concerns that may have popped up during your reading of this book will be addressed.

At this point, you might be wondering who I am and why I think I'm qualified to advise you on the art of bonsai. My name is Clive Woods, and I have been a professional gardener since graduating from high school.

My parents were avid gardeners, and so while my friends spent time riding their bikes and socializing after school, I spent most of my formative years outside in nature. It was inevitable that I would inherit my parents' love of nature and plants, and I soon went on to build a gardening 'empire' of my own.

My specialized interests are in miniature horticulture, meaning both *mini plants* and *mini trees*. Obviously, one of those is bonsai. The second is in microgreens, which you can read about in my other book – *Microgreens: The Insider's Secrets To Growing Gourmet Greens & Building A Wildly Successful Business* co-written with Donny Greens. If you're intrigued by growing miniature forms of common vegetables such as broccoli, radish, and many more, then be sure to check out that book.

My horticultural journey has been exciting, tiring at times but always rewarding. Over the many years I've dedicated to learning and practicing the art of bonsai, I've been blessed to be mentored by some of the best bonsai masters in the U.S. I have made almost all the mistakes there are to make—and you can be sure I've killed my fair share (probably several people's shares!) of bonsai trees.

Now I see it as my duty to give back to the bonsai world that has been so good to me. There is simply no need for the next generation of bonsai growers to make the same mistakes that I and many others have made. Likewise, there is equally no need for as many innocent seedlings and fledging bonsai trees to suffer the same fate that my first bonsai trees suffered. Of course, there is always more for me to learn, but I'm happy to share my considerable body of knowledge with you now.

Everything is set up ready for you—and now it's your turn to act.

American bonsai master John Naka famously once said, "Killing trees is the tuition you pay for learning bonsai."

I believe that it doesn't have to be that way. Yes, you will inevitably make plenty of mistakes while learning how to grow and nurture bonsai trees—especially in the beginning. But I also believe that through knowledge, you can cut the learning curve in half.

So with that, let's get started learning about how not to kill your next bonsai tree!

1

Chapter 1: History & Tradition

Origin of the Word Bonsai

The literal translation of the Japanese word "bonsai" is "planted in a container". The word is also sometimes misspelled in Western countries as "banzai" or "bonzai". While most people assume bonsai originated in Japan, and bonsai is a Japanese word, the practice of growing miniaturized versions of trees has its roots in the mountainous regions of China, where the art of "penjing" predates bonsai techniques by many hundreds of years.

In early Chinese culture, "pen" referred to a pot and "jing" meant landscape or scenery. A penjing was therefore, literally an entire landscape in a pot! This ancient practice was later adopted and localized in Japan as a type of Zen Buddhist practice designed to develop mindfulness and patience among its practitioners.

Origins and Founders

The Chinese art of penjing can be traced back as early as 700 AD, more than 1,300 years ago. At that time, the art of growing miniaturized trees in containers was reserved for elite members of society. Trees were obtained directly from the wild and the final cultivated product was considered a luxurious gift. It's commonly thought that the practice originated in China's harshest mountainous areas where native trees were forced to grow in unique ways in order to survive.

During this time, followers of Taoism (an ancient Chinese philosophy and religion that instructs believers on how to exist in harmony with the universe) are thought to have developed specialized horticultural techniques that allowed them to recreate unique growing patterns of these wild mountain tree species. Certain features of a wild tree—such as a twisted branch—were believed to represent the spirit of sacred animals such as a serpent or dragon. In the 9th Century (the years 801 to 900), the Japanese were known for visiting China and bringing back potted trees to give as prized gifts. This idea of giving bonsai trees as gifts is still practiced today, even in Western culture.

During Japan's Kamakura period (remembered by the introduction of feudalism and the emergence of the samurai) between 1192 to 1333, many aspects of Chinese culture were adopted by Japan, including the Chinese art of penjing. The horticultural techniques that had initially been created by Chinese Taoists were redeveloped by Japanese Zen Buddhists to replicate the fascinating growing patterns of wild Japanese trees. Around this time, Japanese cultural artworks, poetry, and folklore began to include references to miniature trees grown in pots, marking the completion of the assimilation of this element of Chinese culture into Japan. No longer reserved for society's elite, the practice would soon become common among various social classes in Japanese society.

It wasn't until hundreds of years later that the art of bonsai began to spread to the Western world following the occupation of Japan after World War II and the boom of world exhibitions and globalization that followed the end of the war.

The Karate Kid

Arguably one of the most famous and well-known representations of bonsai trees in Western culture is *The Karate Kid* movie series released in the 1980s. These representations began in the first movie, released in

1984, in which the karate master Mr. Miyagi mentors his young student Daniel-san about life and karate philosophy—partially through the art of styling bonsai trees as these trees were shown to represent inner peace and the importance of patience.

In the second Karate Kid movie, released in 1986, less emphasis is placed on bonsai trees as symbolism for life and karate. Only one mention is made, in which Mr. Miyagi refers to a bonsai tree as having a "strong root" and likening the tree to Daniel's inner strength.

Bonsai, however, plays a more significant role in the third Karate Kid movie, released in 1989. Daniel-san is seen establishing his bonsai shop and is shown collecting wild bonsai samples (yamadori) from nature. Mr. Miyagi uses bonsai as a symbol to represent Daniel-san's freedom to create his own karate methods, noting that bonsai "chooses its own way to grow" because its roots are strong.

While bonsai is truly a global phenomenon today, the bulk of bonsai growing continues to take place in China and Japan. At a worldwide level, Asia contains the greatest amount of interest in bonsai growing, followed by Europe and then North America. Interestingly, when Google search trends are considered, the global trend remains relatively constant from 2010 until the start of 2020.

From April 2020 onwards, Google search trends increased dramatically, perhaps pointing to increased interest in bonsai growing while millions of people around the world were forced to spend time at home during the global COVID pandemic.

BONSAI

Chapter 2: Benefits & Amazing Facts

What are Bonsai Trees?

Technically speaking, a bonsai tree is a tree grown in a container. But that does not do justice to this proud art form. In reality, the practice has evolved over the centuries to become a deeply spiritual, meditative practice of applying specialized horticultural techniques to create thriving miniature versions of full-sized trees that would otherwise grow in the wild.

More and more people around the world are beginning to explore the art of bonsai. If you're still questioning whether bonsai is the right venture for you, consider the following reasons to start this fine art form. (We'll touch on physical, spiritual, and health benefits—as well as some reasons why this might also NOT be the perfect hobby for you later in the book).

Suitable for any space: While most bonsai species should be kept outdoors, several species can tolerate indoor living. Examples that thrive indoors include the Ficus, Buddhist Pine, and Dwarf Schefflera. The majority of these three species will fit into almost any space (due to their naturally small stature) so long as they have suitable access to natural light and air (carbon dioxide) for photosynthesis.

Simple to care for: Despite the commonly held misconception that growing a bonsai is challenging, bonsais are relatively simple to care for once you understand the fundamentals. Like with any kind of horticulture, the key to keeping a bonsai tree alive is to understand its individual needs and to be consistent with caring for it, as you'll learn in the chapters that follow.

A generational companion: Bonsai trees can have an incredibly long lifespan. Some of the most famous and valuable bonsai trees in the world today have been passed down through generations and some are estimated to be a thousand years old! The skill you are now learning and the bonsai you begin caring for this year can grow to become a part of your legacy for future generations to maintain and enjoy.

Fostering patience: In Japanese culture, patience is a highly respected virtue. It comes as little surprise that the Japanese people value the art of bonsai for the patience that it fosters. When you gain patience, you develop the ability to tolerate life's annoyances and setbacks without resorting to anger. In today's fast-paced world, patience is a virtue worth cultivating.

Resilience: Bonsai have become a symbol of resilience. Just as trees often struggle to overcome the harshest of conditions to survive in the wild, bonsai trees are often styled to represent struggle and a never-ending will to survive. Many bonsai trees proudly exhibit scars from 'wiring', which we'll learn more about in Chapter 8—as well as other signs of struggle, which add to their beauty.

Selflessness & awareness: Caring for a bonsai involves putting the needs of another living being ahead of your own. So unless you tend to your tree's needs—your tree will fail to thrive. You will also gain an awareness of the seasons and the way your tree responds to different seasons of the year.

The overall practice of growing a bonsai tree can be summarized as fun, relaxing, and entirely addictive, with many people maintaining their bonsai practices for decades after first taking up the hobby. But what are some of the most common lifestyle benefits of growing bonsai trees? Let's take a look.

Many benefits of a pet, without the hassle: If you've considered adding a pet to your life but are unsure about whether you will be able to meet its ongoing needs, a bonsai tree may be an excellent alternative. Bonsai trees bring the benefits of companionship, care, and love, but without many of the more onerous daily hassles involved with having a pet.

Nurture your creativity and artistic side: Nurturing, designing, and creating a bonsai tree is an excellent way of developing your creativity and encouraging your artistic nature to shine. In a very real way, creating a bonsai tree is a collaborative effort between you and your bonsai tree. As a living being, a bonsai tree has its own vision for its direction. At the same time, a bonsai will yield to the wishes of its creator and will bend itself to your will. A bonsai tree is an artistic statement that represents your burgeoning creativity and desired vision for your tree.

Brain training and learning: Just like your body, your brain needs to be used and exercised to avoid decaying. Growing a bonsai tree is an excellent way of keeping your brain active without causing unnecessary levels of stress. There is so much to discover in the field of bonsai. It all depends on how far you wish to take your learning journey.

Brighten the energy in your home: Having a bonsai in your home transforms the energy level inside your living space. You will only truly understand this once you've experienced it for yourself. Those who practice fengshui revere bonsai trees for their ability to positively affect the energy of a room. Meanwhile, almost anyone can affirm that a healthy, well-maintained bonsai tree is a source of happiness and contentment for all who are blessed to share its presence. Of course, this point applies to bonsai species that are kept indoors.

Improved memory: Growing a bonsai tree is an excellent way of improving your memory. As you begin to devote a part of your mind's consciousness to your bonsai tree, you will have to keep track of your tree's needs, including when it was last watered, fertilized, and pruned.

Health Benefits

Not only are bonsai trees a treat to the senses and a delight to behold, but they also offer a range of potential health benefits for growers and for those lucky enough to regularly view a bonsai. Let's explore these benefits now.

Air purification: As trees, bonsais offer the benefit of air purification—despite their miniature stature. Trees and plants release oxygen, thus increasing the aeration of a room while benefitting from the carbon dioxide emitted by us humans to form a symbiotic relationship.

Trains your mind: Caring for a bonsai tree has the innate capability to shift a person's focus away from themselves towards the needs of another living being. As mentioned earlier, this helps train us to become more selfless.

Reduces stress levels: Growing a bonsai tree is an excellent way of reducing your daily stress levels. Bonsai masters tend to agree that spending time communing with nature fosters a feeling of calm, leading to lowered blood pressure, a slower and more stable heart rate, and more relaxed breathing—the perfect way to counter the stresses of ordinary life.

Maintains healthy humidity levels: Bonsai trees, and especially those kept indoors, are excellent at maintaining healthy humidity levels. This can help to reduce the likelihood of dry skin, among other benefits.

Combines our internal and external worlds: Through bonsai, you can begin to understand how your inner world interacts with the external world. When you encounter disappointment, how do you react? Do you come at life's upsets with anger and defeat, or are you able to use logic and understanding to work your way through it? The path to becoming a bonsai master is fraught with hurdles, mistakes, and disappointments. You will inevitably cause damage to your trees and you will regret many of the decisions you make—especially in the early years. But you can choose to see this journey as a safe space in which to observe the way you deal with inevitable setbacks and disappointments.

Growing a bonsai tree is a way of learning to become comfortable with discomfort.

Physical interaction: Creating a bonsai is a physical experience and involves physically interacting with your tree using tools and your own two hands. With so many of today's human interactions taking place behind computer and smartphone screens, it is a refreshing experience and change to become involved in a pursuit that is so hands-on, so to speak.

Symbolism

As touched upon, bonsai trees are a symbol of balance, harmony, and simplicity—integral elements of Japanese culture, both now and for more than a thousand years. Not only does bonsai growing conjure images of spirituality and meaning, but individual tree species also carry their own philosophical symbolism. Let's explore some of these now.

Azalea
   The Azalea tree is a symbol of gentleness, vulnerability, and beauty.
Cherry Blossom
   As the national symbol of Japan, it comes as little surprise that the Cherry Blossom is both culturally and symbolically significant in the world of bonsai. Cherry Blossoms are renowned for their delicate, exceptionally beautiful pink flowers, which last for such a short time each year, usually blossoming around April. As such, the Cherry Blossom has come to symbolize fleeting beauty and the importance of living in the moment.
Chinese Elm
   The Chinese Elm is an ode to love, wisdom, intuition, and inner strength. It is often placed in churches and homes to offer protection to those inside.
Ficus

The Ficus is a symbol of harmony, simplicity, abundance, and new beginnings. It is often referred to as the "cheerful tree" due to its ability to enhance the mood of those around it.

Jade

Jade trees bring a deep association with prosperity and financial success. In fengshui practices, it is common to give a Jade tree to someone starting a new business as a way of wishing them success in their business endeavors.

Japanese Maple

The Japanese Maple is a symbol of beauty and elegance and is highly regarded in Japanese art, culture, and literature.

Juniper

Juniper is a symbol of protection and is thought to ward off evil spirits. Many believe that a Juniper tree has the power to purify and cleanse those around it.

Maple

The Maple tree is a symbol of practicality, serenity, and peace.

Oak

The Oak tree is a symbol of knowledge, strength, and longevity due to its long lifespan and its naturally robust trunk.

Common Myths

Perhaps due to its sacred and mystical perceptions, there are many myths about growing bonsai trees that continue to be perpetuated by the uninformed. In Chapter 11, you'll find a more extensive list of bonsai myths and misconceptions to help you understand how these myths began and why they continue to be widely held today. For now, let's dispel two of the most common myths.

Myth 1: Growing bonsai trees is difficult

This is likely the most common and widespread myth surrounding the art of bonsai tree growing. In reality, growing a bonsai tree is not too dissimilar from any other type of gardening. The key is to understand the individual needs of your tree and to meet those needs. Where bonsai differs is its artistic elements, and this is perhaps where people become wary of bonsai. It is the role of the bonsai grower to have a vision for their tree and to take the necessary steps—including pruning, wiring, and repotting—to achieve their vision. It is this artistic element that is largely missing in other types of horticulture, which is perhaps how the myth that "growing bonsai trees is difficult" continues to be perpetuated.

Myth 2: A Bonsai is a Separate Tree Species
The reality is that when people speak of a "bonsai tree" they are referring to the style and art form of the tree, not a separate tree species such as an apple tree or oak tree. However, it is not uncommon for people to assume that a bonsai tree is its own species—especially when some nurseries and less reputable vendors attempt to sell seeds, seedlings, and trees labeled simply as "bonsai" without any other identifying features.

Did You Know These Amazing Bonsai Facts?

The World's Oldest (Known) Bonsai Trees
The third oldest bonsai tree in the world is a pair of trees located at Japan's Shunkaen Bonsai Museum in Tokyo, both of which are estimated to be more than 800 years old. The second oldest bonsai is a 1,000 year-old Juniper at the Mansei-en bonsai nursery located in Omiya, Japan. The oldest bonsai in the world is thought to be a Ficus that is more than 1,000 years old and was originally cared for by Chinese masters. In 1986 the tree was purchased by the Crespi Bonsai Museum in Italy.

The Age of a Bonsai Tree

The age of a bonsai tree is usually measured by the number of years it has spent growing in a bonsai pot. This means that a tree harvested from the wild—which may itself be several decades old—may end up being "aged" at a lower number of years, beginning from when it starts training inside a bonsai pot.

The World's Most Famous Bonsai

Arguably the world's most famous bonsai is a collection of 11 Juniper trees grown by bonsai master John Naka. Known as "Goshin - Protector of the Spirits," the bonsai collection was created in 1948 to represent the 11 grandchildren of the bonsai master. The collection is now located at the U.S. National Arboretum in Washington D.C.

The World's Largest Bonsai

In official bonsai competitions, the largest size class is known as the Imperial-class for bonsais up to 80 inches tall. However, there is a Red Pine bonsai just under 200 inches tall located in Japan's Shizuoka prefecture. While this bonsai would not qualify for inclusion in the Imperial bonsai class, it can still technically be classified as a bonsai according to the literal definition, which is simply "planted in a container".

The World's Smallest Bonsai

The smallest bonsai class in official competitions is called the Keshitsubo class and is for bonsais between one inch and three inches tall. The smallest bonsai currently known is an Acer Momiji bonsai tree. Caring for a tiny bonsai tree poses unique challenges, as these tiny trees can be extremely sensitive to any changes in climate or condition, as well as requiring a very steady hand and attention to detail!

The Bonsai that Survived the Hiroshima Bombing

A Japanese White Pine bonsai that was cultivated in the 1600s managed to survive the Hiroshima bombings in 1945, despite being located only 2 miles from the detonation zone. In 1975, the bonsai was presented to the United States as a gift, and now lives in the United States National Arboretum. An arboretum, in case you're wondering, is a botanical collection comprised exclusively of trees.

Bonsais that are Harmful to Household Pets

While the art of bonsai is a quiet, peaceful, and reflective practice that provides benefits for growers, some trees may prove harmful to dogs, cats, and other household pets. It is therefore important to keep in mind that bonsai trees are genetically identical to the same tree species grown in the wild. Just as some trees and plants are poisonous to certain animals, their bonsai versions can be equally dangerous as well. For example, Jade trees are poisonous to dogs and can cause vomiting, weakness, and stomach pain. So keep the pups well away!

The World's First Bonsai Convention

The world's first known bonsai convention was the World Bonsai and Suiseki Exhibition held in Osaka, Japan, in 1980.

World Bonsai Day

The second Saturday in May is widely celebrated around the world as World Bonsai Day. This day provides an opportunity for people to come together to share the art of bonsai and participate in competitions and exhibitions.

Bonsai Health Benefits

Bonsai trees are known for their many health benefits, including air purification and access to clean oxygen, a feeling of quiet reflection as you nurture your bonsai over time, and a sense of accomplishment and a job well done when you reap the rewards of your hard work over consecutive years.

Lucky Bonsai

For some people, the benefits of growing bonsai far exceed the potential health benefits. Some people genuinely believe that bonsai trees can bring good luck to their growers, with some going as far as to believe that bonsais hold magical properties. Some bonsai species have their own traditions associated with them. For example, the Jade tree is considered a symbol of financial luck and prosperity, as mentioned earlier. Bonsai trees given as a gift are often thought to be luckier than the same tree purchased for oneself.

Reasons Not to Grow Bonsai

At this stage, it might be useful to discuss some of the biggest reasons not to take on the hobby, so let's take a look at these reasons now.

Constraining a Large Tree Species to a Small Pot is Cruel

It can be argued that since bonsai tree species would naturally grow to their full size in the wild, restricting their growth in a shallow pot is cruel. Indeed, doing so not only restricts their growth but limits their ability to find their own nutrients and water as wild trees normally would. The counter-argument is that bonsai trees are tended to with great care, love, and attention, making up for the restrictions that are placed upon them. It is up to each grower to decide how they feel about this matter.

The Techniques Used to Restrict a Bonsai Tree's Growth are Cruel

Bonsai trees don't just *happen* on their own but are created using specialized horticultural techniques including trimming, pruning, wiring, and root trimming. It is widely accepted that these techniques are highly stressful for the tree, which is why it is advisable only to perform one large operation on your tree each year. More frequent changes could overload the tree's stress system and cause the tree to lose health and potentially die.

The counter-argument is that such trimming and pruning are essential to the health of the tree, allowing it to discard unhealthy elements such as dead or unhealthy branches. However, it must be noted that some changes made to a bonsai tree are purely for stylistic or aesthetic reasons.

If either of these reasons would cause you concern over growing bonsai trees, it may be best to discontinue your studies here. Otherwise, please read on to Chapter 3.

Chapter 3: Types of Bonsai

The knowledge in this chapter will greatly assist you with choosing the best bonsai tree species for starting your journey. In Chapter 12, you'll also find a detailed list of tree species that make excellent bonsai trees, but for now, let's discuss the broad generalities of trees and come to an understanding of some of the primary tree species classifications.

Deciduous, Conifers, Pines, and Broadleaf

Deciduous trees are those that shed their leaves seasonally. Most deciduous trees have broad leaves, making them susceptible to leaf-fall during wet and windy weather conditions. Deciduous trees have adapted to shed their leaves at the onset of the wet weather season, allowing them to better survive harsh weather conditions and to assist in water and energy conservation. The opposite of a deciduous tree is an evergreen tree.

Deciduous trees can be further divided into two primary leaf types: alternating and opposite. Examples of deciduous trees with alternative leaf patterns include Japanese Cherry, Birch, Hornbeam, Japanese Beech, European Beech, and Chinese Elm. Examples of deciduous trees with opposite leaf patterns include the Jacaranda, Trident Maple, and Japanese Maple.

Coniferous trees are those that bear a cone. Pine trees are well-known conifers, as are hemlocks and firs. Most—but notably not all—conifers are woody, evergreen trees and only shed their oldest foliage with no expectation of regrowth. Coniferous trees can be further divided into three primary types: elongating with scale-like leaves, whorled, in which the needles share a common point, and deciduous, in which the needles shed.

Examples of coniferous trees with elongating growth patterns include the Coast Redwood, Japanese Yew, European Spruce, Cedar, and Chinese Juniper. Examples of coniferous trees with whorled growth patterns include the Mountain Pine, Scots Pine, Japanese Red Pine, and Japanese Black Pine. Some examples of coniferous trees with deciduous growth patterns include the Dawn Redwood, Bald Cypress, Japanese Larch, and European Larch.

Broadleaf trees are characterized by broad, relatively flat leaves, often with prominent veins. Broadleaf trees can be further divided into two primary growth patterns: alternating and opposite. Examples of broadleaf trees with alternating leaf patterns include the Cotoneaster, Bougainvillea, Azalea, Fukien Tea, and Fig. Meanwhile, examples of broadleaf trees with opposite leaf patterns include the Acacia, Dwarf Jade, Olive, Honeysuckle, and Boxwood.

At this point, you may be wondering which tree species are best suited to living outdoors, and conversely which species survive well indoors. In Chapter 4, you will find a detailed discussion about the merits of growing bonsai trees indoors versus outdoors, and further in Chapter 12, you'll see an extensive list of various tree species and whether they tolerate indoor care.

In conclusion, while some bonsai trees are easier to grow than others, there is no one simple answer when it comes to choosing the perfect bonsai for a beginner. Much depends on your geographical location, the typical weather and climate in your area, the amount of time and care you can offer your bonsai, and whether you would prefer an indoor or outdoor tree. Within these parameters, the safest choice will always be to select a species that is native to your local area.

Chapter 4: Getting Started

What to Look For and What to Avoid

One of the easiest ways to get started with bonsai growing is to purchase a ready-made bonsai. By taking this action, it allows you to get your hands dirty as soon as possible, without waiting several years for seeds or saplings to germinate.

When choosing a ready-made bonsai, it's best to look for the following positive attributes.

- An **interesting-looking trunk** that tapers from base to top.
- **Evenly spaced surface roots** that appear to naturally enter the soil and support the tree.
- **No branches** on the bottom one-third of the trunk.
- **Varying trunk widths, heights, and spacing** in the case of a group planting.
  When choosing a ready-made bonsai, here are some attributes to avoid.
- A tree that feels **unsecured in its pot** could indicate waterlogged or rotting roots or just an unhealthy tree.
- Anything **labeled as "bonsai seeds"** or a **"bonsai tree"** without any further identifying information as to the specific species of tree.

- Highly packaged bonsais in **boxes or containers** have usually been imported from overseas and are not ideal for your local climate. These trees will usually die.
- **Mottled or yellow foliage** can indicate an unhealthy tree.
- **Prickly trees** will make trimming and handling difficult.
- **Scarring** from previous wiring attempts, as these can take a long time to heal.
- Trees **infested with pests or diseases** should be strictly avoided.
- **Unattractive, crossed, or twisted roots** can be difficult to rectify.

Indoors vs. Outdoors

One of the first and most important considerations to make when choosing a bonsai is whether you intend to keep it indoors or outdoors. Despite the common misconception that bonsai trees are house-bound, it is crucial to understand that all bonsai trees would prefer to spend most—if not all—of their time outdoors. Some bonsai trees, though, can easily tolerate living indoors, so if you plan to keep your bonsai tree indoors, you must select a species that can tolerate an indoor environment.

The most challenging aspect of keeping an indoor bonsai is ensuring that it receives ample sunlight. While your bonsai tree won't die immediately if it doesn't receive enough light, it will fail to thrive. If access to natural sunlight is lacking in your house, you can make use of growing lights to supplement the lack of natural light.

If you're looking for an indoor bonsai, arguably the best and easiest species to look after for a beginner is the Ficus. Not only is the Ficus tolerant of indoor living, but it can also thrive in low humidity and is tolerant of many mistakes that beginners often make.

Starting From Seeds vs. Cuttings

If you're considering growing a bonsai tree from a seed, understand that there is no such thing as a "bonsai seed". A bonsai is not a separate species of tree in the same way that an Apple tree or an Oak tree are considered a distinct species. Thus, be wary of anyone purporting to sell "bonsai seeds" without other identifying information as to the seeds' specific tree species. Without this information, it will be difficult to know how to properly care for your bonsai tree as it matures.

With this in mind, it's certainly possible to grow a bonsai tree from a seed. The primary drawback of this method is that you will need to allow at least two to three years for the seed to grow into a large enough tree to start applying bonsai growing techniques. If you're eager to begin learning the art of growing bonsai straight away, it's better to start from an existing bonsai tree rather than starting from a seed.

Another alternative is to start by cultivating a cutting from an existing tree. Known as "sashiki" in Japanese, growing a bonsai from a cutting is an inexpensive and rewarding way to get started with bonsai. As with growing a bonsai from a seed, you won't be able to begin pruning and shaping your bonsai for several years until it has grown sufficient in size. However, the wait time will be significantly shortened if starting from a cutting rather than a seed.

Growing a bonsai from either a seed or a cutting will be an early test of your patience. You may like to work on existing bonsai trees at the same time as you wait for your seed or cutting to grow.

Grafting

Grafting—or "tsugiki" in Japanese—is the method of fusing a root, branch, or shoot to a tree. The idea behind grafting is to combine the best qualities of two different trees into one tree, to replace foliage with that of another tree variety, to improve surface roots by adding additional roots, or to create a new tree by combining the best qualities of two existing trees.

There are three different grafting methods: scion grafting, approach grafting, and thread grafting.

Scion grafting involves inserting a separate graft into the branch or trunk of a tree. **Approach grafting** involves using a donor plant with intact roots and attaching it to a receiving tree. With **thread grafting**, a hole is drilled through the branch or trunk of a tree, and a branch of another tree is inserted through the hole. Scion and thread grafting are best completed in late Winter before the trees begin to grow, while approach grafting usually gives the best results in Summer.

For grafting to be successful, both trees must be of the same species. After the grafting process is complete, it becomes an exercise in patience to see if the graft has been successful. Your bonsai tree should be left untouched for the remainder of the growing season and only checked for success the following Spring.

Sourcing From a Store, Online, or Nature?

Sourcing a bonsai from a store—whether in person or online—can be a daunting process. The trick is to find a reputable seller who is knowledgeable about bonsai trees and who isn't trying to make easy money by selling low-quality imported stock to unsuspecting novices. As mentioned above, be wary of anyone trying to sell "bonsai seeds" or "bonsai trees" as if a bonsai were a separate species of tree.

Many plant nurseries will have young trees available for purchase. Called pre-bonsai, these young trees can be both an affordable and rewarding way to get started in the art of bonsai. Make sure that you are provided with details about the tree species before you buy and ensure that you understand the tree's optimal growing conditions before you take it home.

As a general tip, smaller nurseries often have better quality stock (and more knowledgeable staff) than larger chain-store style nurseries—though this isn't always the case.

It's also possible to source bonsai trees online, although extreme care must be taken. Check to make sure that the store shows photos of the actual tree you will be receiving, not just a sample of what a particular species could look like if grown successfully. Take the time to find reputable sellers with excellent online feedback. New sellers or those with negative or mixed reviews should be avoided.

Another way of sourcing bonsai stock is to cultivate them directly from the wild. In Japanese, "yamadori" refers to a tree that has naturally grown in a miniaturized (bonsai) version, usually due to a lack of nutrients or sunlight. While this can be an excellent source of quality bonsai trees, extreme care must be taken. In many areas, it is against the law to relocate trees from national parks, forests, and other public areas. Always seek permission from the landowner or parkkeeper before removing any vegetation.

If you are granted permission, make sure you have all your tools and equipment on hand and are ready with a pot and appropriate bonsai soil at home. When digging out the tree, take a generous portion of the surrounding soil to not damage the root system during the relocation process.

Transforming a Mature Tree or Shrub into a Bonsai

Converting a mature tree or shrub into a bonsai is very common and a cheap way to hone your bonsai skills. After selecting a target specimen from a nursery or your own garden, you will need to clean the tree by removing dead or weak branches that can't be used with your design, small and weaker green branches in the interior of a dense canopy that clog up space around established branches (that will be later wired and styled), as well as bottom growing branches that conceal the lower trunk.

As a result of this cleaning work, you will have more space to see and familiarize yourself with the underlying structure of the tree, including various nuances, before you later start the design and style process. First, though, you need to decide on the front of the tree. This decision should generally be based on maximizing the shape and movement of the trunkline (i.e. bends and curves).

Before cleaning   After cleaning

Before cleaning   After cleaning

Next, you will need to remove the tree from the original container to a special bonsai pot, which depending on how established the root system is, can be a delicate or a relatively easy operation. If you find that the tree is adhering to the exterior walls of the container, you can use a chopstick or a serrated cutting blade to cut the roots that are in contact with the wall of the container. Once the tree is separated from the existing pot, you can loosen the existing soil from the roots, trim the roots back, select your soil using the knowledge you learned in Chapter 6, and follow the tips for repotting a tree outlined in Chapter 9. Remember, too, that process of repotting your pre-bonsai tree offers you an opportunity to establish a new angle for the trunk.

In terms of selecting a tree to convert to a bonsai, a conifer or deciduous tree can be a good option for beginners, but you can also choose any of the trees mentioned in this book. In general, you want to first look for a tree that interests you, such as fleshy leaves, interesting branches, or a maybe structure that reminds you of a tree in your backyard as a kid. Then, you want to look for a tree with a good base, such as a thick trunk or a trunk that changes directions with different spaces between each branch. Ultimately, your chosen tree should inspire a vision of something grander and more artistic once cared for under bonsai growing techniques.

Pots

An appropriate pot is an essential aspect of growing a bonsai. In the next chapter, you will find a detailed explanation of the different types of pots that can be suitable for bonsai trees and a guide on how to choose the best pot for your tree.

For now, it's sufficient to say that the number one consideration to make when choosing a bonsai pot is that the pot must be deep enough to sustain the tree and provide it with a healthy living environment. A second consideration is that the pot you choose for your bonsai should be simple and understated in its design, in order to always remain subordinate to your tree. The tree must be the focal point of your display and should never need to compete with its pot for visual attention.

Bringing a new bonsai tree home can be an obstacle. Many new bonsais die in the first season after being acquired—simply because they are incapable of adapting to their new growing conditions. The most important consideration in maximizing the chances of keeping your new bonsai tree alive is finding the ideal location to place your tree. This decision must be guided by the tree species and its particular needs. A tree that must live outdoors simply won't be able to thrive indoors, and a tree that requires partial shade will fail to survive long-term under full sunlight. Thoroughly research the tree species you've chosen and check that you are well-equipped to care for your new tree.

Once you bring your new bonsai tree home, it is best to avoid any major styling, repotting, or shaping procedures until the following Spring. Make sure your bonsai is well watered but avoid fertilizing it until its first growing season. By leaving your bonsai largely alone for the first few seasons, you give it the best chance of acclimatizing to its new environment and becoming properly established before making any major changes to it.

5

Chapter 5: Tools & Equipment

Bonsai Tools, Uses, and Prices

When working with bonsai trees, it is vitally important to have access to the right type of tools and equipment. As miniature versions of full-sized trees, bonsais are sensitive and as such, require specialized tools to make each task as clean and straightforward as possible.

Rather than purchasing a complete set of bonsai tools at the outset, beginners should start with the most essential tools they will need right away, like concave cutters and shears. As your experience level grows and you come across new growing scenarios, you can purchase the right tools as required. Ensure that you only use your bonsai tools for their intended task, keep them well maintained, and stored properly. That way, your bonsai tools will last you for many years to come.

The following is a list of bonsai tools, including prices, listed in alphabetical order.

Bonsai pruning shears allow you to remove small and intermediate branches, twigs, leaves, and root pruning.

Japanese stainless steel - 200mm to 210mm - approximately $US 40 to $US 67

Japanese carbon steel - 200mm - approximately $US 30

Bowls are useful for root work or to mix new batches of bonsai soil.

Branch cutters (and branch splitters) are sharp pliers used to split stumps and dead branches.

Japanese stainless steel - 180mm to 280mm - approximately $US 47 to $US 117

Japanese carbon steel - 180mm to 210mm - approximately $US 40 to $US 55

Bud scissors are used for trimming small branches, buds, and leaves.

Carving tools are used for shaping, contouring, smoothing, and otherwise working with deadwood.

Japanese stainless steel - approximately $US 37

Chopsticks are useful to avoid air pockets by pushing bonsai soil between and under the roots.

Concave pruners are arguably the most important bonsai tool. They are used to remove branches in a way that will not leave a lasting wound or scar.

Japanese stainless steel - approximately $US 32

Disinfectants should always be used to clean your bonsai tools in order to prevent transporting bacteria or infections from one tree to another.

Electric bonsai tools are available and can be used to smooth deadwood, remove bark, and other similar tasks. However, it is recommended that bonsai growers perfect the art of manually completing these tasks using more traditional and authentic tools before trying their hand at electric tools.

A **gas torch** can be helpful for removing wood fibers following a trimming session. You will also need some lighter fluid too.

A **grindstone** is used to sharpen the blades of your various bonsai tools.

Jin pliers are similar to branch splitters but are used when working on the less fibrous wood of deciduous trees or conifers.

Japanese stainless steel - approximately $US 50

Japanese carbon steel - approximately $US 35

Knob cutters are a good bonsai tool to own, even though they might be used less than concave pruners or bud scissors. Knob cutters are uniquely shaped to bite into knobs of wood with ease and execute a clean cut that will heal over the course of time. They therefore allow for the easy removal of unwanted areas of the trunk or roots.

Japanese stainless steel - 180mm to 210mm - approximately $US 47 to $US 56

Japanese carbon steel - 180mm to 210mm - approximately $US 37 to $US 40

Loop knives (and carving hooks) can be used to carve furrows and peel off sections of bark.

Raffia, rubber tape, and rubber tubes are helpful to protect a branch before bending. Using rubber or raffia protection helps prevent the bark from tearing or the wood from breaking when restyling or before wiring.

A **rainwater tank** may be necessary if your main water supply contains a heavy concentration of chlorine or limescale. Call your supplier and ask them to send you the water parameters.

Root cutters (or root scissors) are used to shorten or remove large roots. These tools are at risk of damage due to the likelihood of small rocks or stones becoming caught in the blades. These tools can also be used to prune branches that are too thick for concave pruners.

Japanese stainless steel - 195mm to 270mm - approximately $US 45 to $US 80

Japanese carbon steel - 195mm to 210mm - approximately $US 32

Root hooks (and root rakes) are useful when opening the bonsai's root ball, removing old soil from the roots, and combing the roots. Bamboo chopsticks can be used for smaller bonsai trees, while a root hook or root rake is more suitable for medium and large bonsai trees.

Japanese stainless steel - 220mm to 255mm - approximately $US 21 to $US 27

Rusk erasers can be used to maintain your bonsai tools by removing dirt and rust.

A **saw** is used to cut roots, tree trunks, and branches that are too hard or thick for other tools.

Japanese stainless steel - 180mm - approximately $US 20

Scoops are used to fill soil into the bonsai pot and are specially designed to ensure that soil is evenly distributed under low-hanging branches.

Sickle knives and saws are tools specifically designed to assist in removing a root ball from a pot.

A **sieve** can help to separate different sizes of grain from granular bonsai soil and to remove the smallest dust particles.

A **slim chisel** can be used to lift wood fibers as needed.

Spray cans are helpful when applying water, leaf fertilizer, or plant protection in a misting fashion.

A **turntable** can protect your workspace from scratches when turning your bonsai trees during trimming and pruning.

Tweezers (and tweezer spatulas) can be used to excavate weeds, apply wet moss to the bonsai soil, remove debris and fallen leaves from the surface of the soil, and grasp tiny items like leaves and twigs.

A **watering can/wand** will become one of your most-used bonsai tools. Look for one with a long neck and a fine nozzle to achieve adequate pressure.

Wire is necessary when it comes time to shape your bonsai. Beginners tend to find aluminum wire easier to work with, while copper wire is another option for more experienced growers.

Wire cutters are used to cut lengths of wire when applying it to a bonsai—but more importantly, they can be used to remove the wire after the bonsai has been trained. By this stage, the wire will be in close contact with the branch or trunk and needs to be removed with utmost care. Bonsai wire cutters have exceptionally short blades and have been specifically designed to remove shaping wire without harming the tree.

Japanese stainless steel - 120mm to 210mm - approximately $US 21 to $US 55

Japanese carbon steel - 180mm - approximately $US 35

Wood hardener is useful when attempting to preserve decayed deadwood. Japanese versions often contain lime sulfur that can whiten deadwood while simultaneously preserving it.

Choosing a Bonsai Pot

A bonsai tree and its pot are inextricably linked. No matter how beautiful and well cared for a bonsai tree may be, if it's in the wrong pot, its full potential will likely be hampered. A bonsai tree will not be able to reach its full potential until it is planted in the right bonsai pot.

Contrary to popular belief, the right bonsai pot does not need to be Japanese, nor does it need to be expensive. As long as a pot meets a few basic requirements, such as having drainage holes and wiring holes, any pot could potentially work. Choosing the right pot comes down to understanding the importance of the pot's material, size, color, and other factors—as well as how they relate to your tree.

Material

Classic bonsai pots are typically constructed from porcelain or ceramic and are stoneware burned. This ensures that the pot itself cannot absorb or hold water within itself. Other materials such as plastic, concrete, and certain metals can also be suitable for a bonsai pot. If considering a metal container, be aware that some metals may release toxins, which is not suitable.

Size

The dimensions of a bonsai pot are arguably its most important attribute. To measure your pot, first check the width of the tree above the soil or the nebari (surface roots). This is going to be the target height of your pot. If you think that this sounds short, you are absolutely right. Bonsai pots are typically short and wide. In terms of the width of the pot, this will depend on whether the pot is oval/rectangular or round. The width of oval or rectangular pots should be two-thirds of the height of the tree, while the diameter of a round pot should be one-third the height of the tree.

Masculine and Feminine Trees/Pots

The next step is to determine whether your tree is masculine or feminine. Most trees contain a mixture of masculine and feminine elements, so it is up to you to determine the most important and obvious elements of your tree to emphasize.

Masculine trees are strong-looking, perhaps with old-looking, mature, or craggy bark, a thick or heavily tapered trunk, deadwood, a dense canopy, and dense or strongly angular branches. Masculine trees often have shari (a vertical section of the tree's trunk without bark) or jin (an area of a branch that has been stripped away, mimicking the effects of age, lightning, or strong wind) as part of their design.

Feminine trees are those with a delicate appearance, perhaps with some curves, a sense of grace, sparse branches, a smooth trunkline, a slow taper, a light or rounded canopy, and smooth bark.

Now that you've decided whether to consider your tree masculine or feminine, it's time to choose a pot to match. Masculine pots tend to be deeper and more angular, with stout feet and clean lines. Its rim may have a prominent lip. Feminine pots are those with softer lines that are sleek and relatively low, usually with delicate feet. Androgenous pots are suitable for either masculine or feminine trees and have rounded or drum-style pots.

Color and Glaze

When choosing the color of your pot, look first to find a color that compliments some element of your tree. Look to the tree's fruit or flowers, the bark color, or the color of its leaves, and seek to match this color in your pot. This makes unglazed earth tones—including brown and grey—a safe choice. Such colors provide stability and warmth to the overall appearance of the tree.

As an alternative, choosing contrasting colors like green and blue can refresh the composition of your tree/pot combination and provide balance to the overall look.

If in doubt about whether to choose a glazed or unglazed pot, be aware that unglazed is always a safe choice. Most evergreen bonsai trees look best in an unglazed pot. Glazed pots look best with fruit or flower-bearing trees and deciduous trees. Remember to choose a pot that isn't too glaring or attention-bearing, as you want the tree to be the focal point.

The texture of the pot should again reflect the masculinity or femininity of your tree. Feminine trees are best suited to smooth clay pots, while pots with heavy textures should be reserved for masculine trees.

Expensive vs. Cheap Equipment

Purchasing your first bonsai tools can be a daunting process. When comparing various versions of a single tool, you will inevitably find seemingly identical versions of a tool with remarkably different price tags. Genuine Japanese-made tools can be expensive, while similar-looking tools made in China may be significantly cheaper. This raises the question: as a beginner, should you spend a large sum of money on your first set of tools, or is it better to start with cheaper tools and upgrade as you gain experience?

This decision is ultimately a personal one. To help you decide, consider the fact that cheaper tools will require more ongoing maintenance as they will be more likely to develop rust. More expensive tools are generally made from stainless steel, which requires less maintenance as they are less likely to rust—meaning they will last longer.

An alternative to buying cheap tools is to look for second-hand versions of more expensive brands. Although the tools will have been used before, as long as they have been well looked after, they will still bring all the advantages of the more expensive tools.

Supporting Small Businesses

Regardless of whether you choose to purchase expensive Japanese crafted bonsai tools or cheaper tools, it's still a good idea to build your set of bonsai tools one at a time rather than purchasing an entire kit.

Every aspect of growing bonsai should be mindful, and this includes purchasing your tools. It is best to buy each tool mindfully and purposefully as you need it, rather than buying an entire kit of tools upfront without fully appreciating what each tool is designed to do.

In the same vein, it is preferable to purchase your bonsai tools from a locally run business rather than a chain-style department store or an on-line conglomerate. If you are lucky enough to have access to a local store that stocks quality bonsai tools and that employs staff with in-depth knowledge of the art of bonsai, they deserve your support and patronage. They will also likely be a valuable source of advice and support in your future bonsai growing endeavors.

Chapter 6: Planting & Soiling

Location and Light

In Chapter 4, we discussed the difference between growing trees indoors versus outdoors, as well as the importance of understanding which bonsai species tolerate indoor living and those that cannot. With this distinction in mind, it is vital to consider your bonsai tree's light requirements and how best to meet these requirements in either environment. Keep in mind that a lack of light will significantly affect the health of your bonsai, slowing down its growth until it ultimately dies.

Indoor Bonsais

Most indoor bonsai species are subtropical trees that require high levels of humidity and plenty of sunlight. Not only will an indoor bonsai require a prime location in front of a window that receives plenty of sunlight, but it will also need to be located as close to the window as possible. Light intensity drops remarkably with every inch that you move away from the window.

There is always the possibility that your indoor bonsai is not receiving sufficient light, even if it is placed right next to the sunniest window available. Fortunately, artificial grow lights can be used to supplement your tree's daily light requirements. Alternatively, consider placing your indoor bonsai outdoors for a few hours each day to supplement its sunlight.

To meet an indoor bonsai tree's humidity requirements, you may need to use a humidity tray. Choose an area of your home with a relatively consistent temperature.

Outdoor Bonsais

Outdoor bonsai trees tend to have high requirements for sunlight, just like their full-sized counterparts growing in the wild. While each tree's specific sunlight needs will vary, as a guide, consider that your bonsai will need 10 hours a day of sunlight. You may need to move your bonsai around between different locations to achieve optimal lighting conditions.

Outdoor bonsais also need to experience the full annual cycle of seasons. This means that they will need to experience Winter dormancy (see Chapter 10 for more details on Winter-proofing your bonsai) and won't require as much sunlight during that time.

Forest/Group Planting

Most bonsai trees are planted alone in a pot. Not only is this the traditional method of creating and displaying bonsai, but it is also what is most commonly depicted in cultural and media references to bonsai trees. However, in nature, trees generally appear in groups. Since the art of bonsai is intended to replicate nature—albeit in miniature form—it stands to reason that group planting would exist in bonsai form. In Japanese, "yose-ue" refers to a group planting of bonsai trees.

The trick to creating a forest or group bonsai planting is to curate the perfect set of trees. Ideally, your group planning will feature trees of one species but varying in size, shape, age, and thickness of their trunks. The beauty of forest planting is its natural realism. It is commonly noted that a well-created bonsai forest gives the viewer the impression that tiny birds could naturally fly through the branches.

Most group plantings include an odd number of trees—generally between five and fifteen. A primary tree is identified—typically the strongest, most dominant tree in the set. This tree should be planted in the center of the planter tray and remain as the focal point of your planting.

Next, a shorter tree known as an annex tree should be placed behind and to the left of the primary tree. A third, even shorter tree should then be planted towards the back right. This tree is known as the jumper tree. The remainder of the trees should then be planted in your desired positions at varying distances. Importantly, ensure that each of the trunks can be viewed in its entirety when viewing the forest from the front.

Introduction to Aqua Bonsai

Aqua bonsai is an exciting new development in the world of bonsai gardening, combining the theory of hydroponics with the art of bonsai trees. Hydroponics involves growing plants and trees solely in water without the use of soil of any kind.

When applied to bonsai trees, aqua bonsai is the practice of growing bonsai trees by submerging their roots in water, instead of bonsai soil. One difficulty with aqua bonsai is avoiding the roots from rotting due to their constant submersion in water. This is achieved largely by changing the water regularly (typically every week) and by adding supplements to the water to ensure the tree receives all the nutrients it needs to survive.

Detailed methods of growing and caring for aqua bonsai are beyond the scope of this book. Aqua bonsai remains an exciting new development that is sure to capture the imaginations of some adventurous bonsai growers.

Soil and Drainage

The right soil mixture for your trees is vitally important. As will be discussed later in Chapter 7 in the section on fertilization, bonsai trees are necessarily restricted in their natural efforts to locate nutrients in the soil using the roots. It is down to the bonsai grower to provide the perfect mixture of nutrients in the right type of bonsai soil to ensure the success of a bonsai tree's growth and survival.

Bonsai soil serves several purposes. Not only does it—in addition to fertilizer—provide a bonsai tree with essential nutrients, but it also must retain water in the right proportions while draining sufficiently to avoid root rot and provide aeration to the tree. Aeration and drainage are especially important, which is why specific ingredients go into bonsai soil that are not found in typical potting mix or garden soil. The ingredients used to create a bonsai mix must be large enough to allow for air pockets between each particle, providing essential oxygen for the roots and allowing for the formation of beneficial bacteria.

Despite being known as bonsai "soil", there is typically no actual soil in a bonsai soil mix. Bonsai soil is closer to gravel than organic soil. Instead, the following elements are common.

Akadama is a Japanese clay that has been specifically created to grow bonsai trees.

Pumice is a type of volcanic rock that absorbs nutrients and water very well.

Lava rock further helps with water retention and aids in the overall structure of the bonsai soil mixture.

The specific proportions of akadama, pumice, and lava rock will vary between tree species, making it once again important for you to understand the particular needs of your tree species.

As a general guide, deciduous trees perform well with a mix that is two parts akadama to one part pumice and one part lava rock, while conifers and pine species may prefer equal parts akadama, pumice, and lava rock.

Chapter 7: Fertilizing & Watering

Water

One of the most important aspects of caring for any bonsai tree is of course watering. As with almost any type of vegetation (or human), if your bonsai tree isn't watered correctly, it will eventually die.

Unlike houseplants, bonsai trees must never be watered on a one-size-fits-all schedule. Instead, consider various factors such as the size and species of your tree, the size of its pot, your local climate, whether your bonsai is indoors or outdoors, and the time of year to know when and how often to water it.

Understanding When Your Bonsai Needs Watering

The key to watering a bonsai tree is to do so when the bonsai soil begins to feel slightly dry. Never water a bonsai tree in wet soil, but likewise, never allow your bonsai soil to dry out completely.

Understanding the right time to water your bonsai takes practice. Start by using your finger to feel the condition of the soil at about half an inch below the surface. With practice, you will be able to visually tell the condition of the soil without touching it—most experienced growers will learn to tell when a bonsai needs watering by feeling the weight of the pot.

The pot will also typically feel lighter when the soil is dry. When you notice the soil drying out, water your bonsai and ensure that the root mass is thoroughly wet. Don't water your bonsai again until the soil shows signs of becoming dry.

Coping with a Heat Wave

Trees not only become dormant but can also shut down and die in hot temperatures (that deviate from other periods of the year), which makes it critical to prepare for hot weather using the following strategies.

First, watering before the temperatures rises will help to prevent the tree from drying out during a heat wave. When the temperature does rise, you can also cool down your tree between watering by lightly sprinkling the tree a further three times a day. If you are using a hose, be careful when you turn on the hose as the initial release of water can be very hot. Also, be on the watch for fungus developing—especially when watering in the afternoon—as warm weather is conducive to fungus growth and it's best to avoid spraying fungicides or pesticides during a heat wave.

Second, move your tree away from fences, walls, or other structures that reflect light and heat. Instead, look for corners, large overhanging trees, or other parts of the garden where there's less direct sun exposure in order to shade your tree.

Third, you can protect the top of the soil and prevent the surface roots from drying out by adding a layer of white sphagnum moss or mountain moss. Moving a tree to the ground and rotating the pot so that the foliage casts shade on the pot can help to prevent the roots from overheating. Additionally, you can shield the roots from overheating by moving pots closer together (to provide shade for each other), turning the tree so lower branches shade the pot, or resting a board against the pot to provide shade. Some bonsai growers also wrap their pots in a wet towel or aluminum foil to reflect heat from the pot, or lay burlap sacks or a light color fabric around the pot.

If you suddenly discover that your tree is distressed by the heat, you should water it so that the rootball is wet and then mist the tree and water again when the soil shows signs of drying out.

Finally, if heat spikes are common in your area and you have a sizeable collection of trees, you may want to consider installing a shade cloth and/or using larger pots for growing that offer better insulation from the heat.

How to Water a Bonsai

The **immersion method** is the perfect way to water a bonsai tree. This method involves submerging the pot fully into a container of water so that the entire pot and the base of the tree's trunk are completely submerged. Stale air in the soil will bubble out, which will be replaced by fresh air when the soil drains.

You should leave the pot submerged for about 10 minutes to ensure all stale air has completely escaped. As you gently remove the pot from the container of water, you will notice fresh air being drawn into the bonsai soil as much of the water drains out of the pot's drainage holes. While this technique might seem unusual, it is highly effective.

Fertilizer

Trees growing naturally in the wild are very adept at using their complex root systems to search for all the nutrients they need in the soil. Bonsai trees, confined to their small pots, are fully reliant on their growers to provide the nutrients they would otherwise have sourced in the wild. Therefore, fertilizing your bonsai is crucial for its survival.

BONSAI

The Elements of Bonsai Fertilizer

All fertilizers designed for bonsai trees must contain three crucial elements:

Nitrogen (N) promotes the growth of leaves and stems.

Phosphorus (P) promotes root growth and boosts the growth of flowers and fruits.

Potassium (K) promotes the overall growth and healthfulness of the tree.

Other optional elements in bonsai fertilizers can include copper, zinc, molybdenum, boron, manganese, and iron.

Buying a bonsai fertilizer mix online or from a local nursery is your best option here.

Fertilizing Different Types of Bonsai

Indoor and subtropical bonsai trees rely on a balanced liquid fertilizer, which should be applied year-round given that indoor and subtropical bonsai trees do not experience seasonal changes. Bonsai trees growing outdoors tend to perform better when the makeup of their fertilizer changes with the seasons.

In the **Spring**, use a formulation with high Nitrogen content, such as an NPK ratio of 10:6:6.

During the **Summer**, a balanced formulation with an NPK ratio of 1:1:1 is recommended.

In the **Fall**, use a formulation with low Nitrogen content, such as an NPK ratio of 3:6:6.

During the **Winter** months, you won't need to fertilize your outdoor bonsai.

Young trees tend to grow much more rapidly than older trees and thus require more frequent fertilizing. Older trees are usually fertilized less often than younger trees.

Deciduous bonsai trees should be fertilized every week during the growing season, with fertilizing ceased once the tree's leaves have fallen.

On the other hand, conifers generally need to be fertilized weekly during the growing season and sparingly during Winter. Conifers can benefit from an NPK ratio fertilizer of 0:10:0 during Fall and Winter.

Tips for Fertilizing Your Bonsai

- It is always better to under-fertilize a tree than to over-fertilize it. If in doubt as to whether you should fertilize your tree, err on the side of caution.
- Only healthy, growing, and established trees should be fertilized. Never fertilize a sick or dormant tree.
- Remember that different tree species have unique fertilization requirements. Ensure that you know your tree's species and needs before beginning a fertilization regime.
- Fertilizer should never be added to dry soil. Ensure that you water your bonsai immediately before fertilizing.

Chapter 8: Styling, Shaping, Wiring & Pruning

Styling and Shaping

Several bonsai styles have emerged over the long history of the art, most of which are designed to resemble natural tree formations. Let's take a look at some of them here. Stunning, beautiful, and awe-inspiring come to mind!

Broom (Hokidachi): Perfect for deciduous trees, the broom style features a straight, upright trunk that begins branching out in multiple directions at one-third of the tree's height.

Formal Upright (Chokkan): The formal style is defined by the visible tapering of an upright trunk which is thicker at the bottom and gradually becomes thinner. Branching begins at about one-quarter of the trunk's length.

Informal Upright (Moyogi): When a tapered trunk grows in roughly an "S" shape with branching at every turn, this is known as the informal upright style.

Leaning/Slanting (Shakkan): In nature, the leaning/slanting style naturally occurs when a tree grows in a shadow and must bend to reach the sun, or when a tree grows in the face of a persistent heavy wind. In bonsai style, this phenomenon is replicated by styling the tree at an angle between 60 and 80 degrees from the ground.

Cascade (Kengai): In nature, when falling rocks or heavy snow persistently put pressure on a tree, it can begin to cascade downwards. In bonsai style, this look can be difficult to maintain as it opposes the tree's natural growing tendencies. When it is pulled off, however, the aesthetics are tremendous.

Semi-Cascade (Han Kengai): Similar to the cascade style, the semi-cascade style is most commonly seen on riverbanks and cliffs. The trunk begins growing upwards and then grows sideways but without dipping below the bottom of the pot.

Literati (Bunjingi): In nature, literati trees are those that grow in areas densely populated with trees. To receive sufficient sunlight, the tree will seek to reach higher heights than its neighbors. The lower portion of the tree is left without branches and often even without bark.

Windswept (Fukinagashi): Similar to a leaning/slanting bonsai, a windswept bonsai features a sideways-growing trunk with all branches leaning to one side of the tree.

Double Trunk (Sokan): When two trunks grow out of a single root system, or one trunk grows out of a larger trunk just above the top of the soil, this is known as the double trunk style.

Multi Trunk (Kabudachi): Similar to the double trunk style, a multi-trunk bonsai is one where three or more trunks grow out of a single root system and form one crown of foliage.

Forest/Group Planting (Yose Ue): A group planting of multiple separate bonsai trees. The most mature trees are planted in the center of the pot, with smaller, less developed trees planted in a staggered arrangement on the outside of the pot. All trees contribute to a single foliage crown. Refer back to Chapter 6 for more details on how to achieve this style.

Rock Planting (Seki Joju): When the roots of a tree grow over a rock before entering the bonsai soil, this is known as rock planting. This style has been created to resemble trees that naturally extend their roots into rocks to search for nutrients.

Growing on Rock (Ishisuki): When trees grow in the cracks and gaps between rocks, they are extremely limited in their efforts to find water and nutrients. Bonsai plants grown in this style are usually purposefully deprived of nutrients to illustrate that they have had to struggle to survive.

Raft (Ikadabuki): When a tree has been cracked in nature, it can sometimes continue to survive by pointing its branches in an upward direction. Over time, the old branches develop into trunks and create branches of their own, with all branches contributing to a single foliage canopy.

Deadwood (Sharimiki): As a result of harsh climatic conditions, some trees develop areas where their bark is sparse or bald. These areas eventually become bleached as a result of sunlight exposure. In bonsai form, this style can be created by deliberately removing sections of bark and bleaching the bald areas with lime sulfur.

These are the most common styles of bonsai shaping, but there are many more to explore. We recommend taking a look on Pinterest for more ideas, should these not be enough for you! My personal favorite style is the Moyogi (informal upright) style, because of its simplistic beauty.

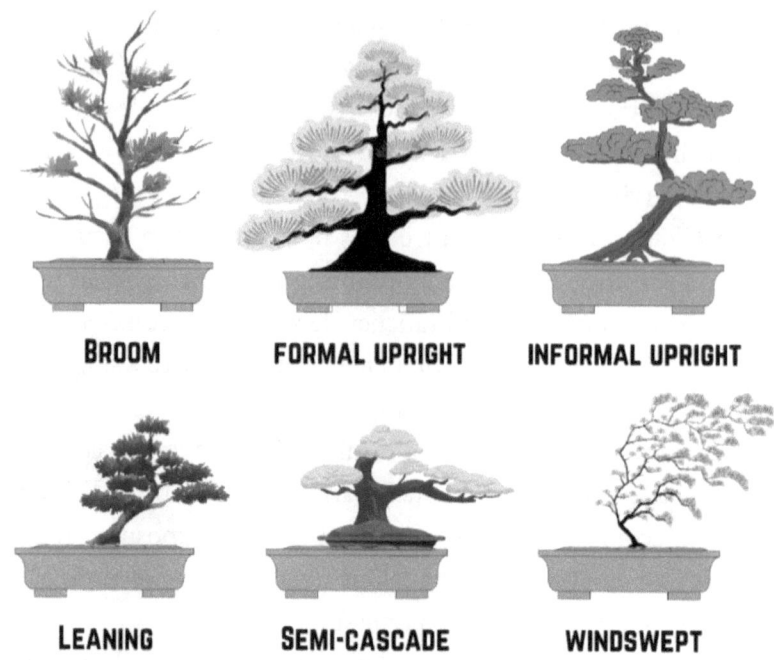

Apical Dominance

Before exploring the ideas of pruning and root trimming, it is helpful to understand the way trees naturally grow in the wild. In general, trees will favor their central stem over their side stems when growing—a phenomenon known as *apical dominance*. The central stem of a tree's branch will grow with more dominance than the twigs and offshoots on the sides of the branch. Apical dominance has evolved to allow trees to grow taller rather than wider, giving them a competitive advantage over neighboring trees.

By understanding apical dominance, you can better understand how to prune your tree to counter this natural tendency. Since your bonsai will favor growth on its central stems, it is important to concentrate your pruning efforts on the outer and top portions of the tree, forcing it to redistribute its growing efforts to its lower and inner areas.

Wiring

Wiring is an essential skill to style and train your bonsai tree. Wiring allows you to reposition and redirect the trunk and branches of your tree by wrapping wire and maneuvering the tree into your desired position. A few months later, the branches will have set in their new position, and the wire can be removed.

When to Wire Your Bonsai

Deciduous trees perform best when wired during Winter, as it is easier to perform the wiring task when there are fewer leaves on the tree. Otherwise, trees can be wired at any time of the year. Be mindful when wiring during your tree's growing season, as the fast spurts of growth can cause the tree to grow into the wire at a faster rate than normal. If the wire is left on too long, the bark of the tree can begin to grow around the wire, which can potentially cause scarring.

Types of Bonsai Wire

Bonsai wire is available in two types: annealed copper and anodized aluminum. Aluminum wire is more manageable for beginners to work with and is particularly recommended for deciduous trees. For more experienced wire handlers, copper wire is recommended for pines and conifers.

Bonsai wire comes in a variety of thicknesses from 1mm to 8mm. It is generally advisable to choose a wire that is one-third the thickness of the branch. Thick wire should be wrapped in water-soaked raffia before being applied to the tree.

How to Wire Your Bonsai Tree

The wiring process begins by cutting off a length of wire sufficiently long to wrap around the trunk twice and then wrapping around the desired branch with even spacing and at a consistent angle of 45 degrees from base to tip. This angle allows the branch to continue to grow thicker in its new position.

If you intend to bend a branch in a downward direction, ensure that the wiring comes from below the branch. Conversely, if you'd like the branch to bend upwards, ensure that the wiring comes from above the branch.

Once you have wired each branch, it is time to start repositioning the branches to create independent paths. Use your fingers to perform this task by pinching the wire down as your wrap it in place, keeping in mind that each branch should only be repositioned once. Moving a branch multiple times increases the risk of the branch becoming damaged. In addition, avoid cranking the wire around the branches too tightly.

Before you start wiring a living tree, it's worthwhile practicing on a dead branch locked into a vice. After practicing, you can deliberately try to break/snap the dead branch as this process will inform you how much pressure will break the branch as well as the feeling just before it breaks.

Removing the Wire

Depending on the time of year and your specific bonsai tree species, it will take between one and four months for the branches to grow around the wiring. Ensure that you remove the wires before the bark begins growing around them. Never try to unwrap wire from the branches, as this is highly likely to cause damage to the bark. Instead, use bonsai wire cutters to snip the wire at every turn. This will make your job much easier.

Pruning

Pruning is the primary way for bonsai trees to be trained. Maintenance pruning refines the existing shape of an already-trained bonsai while encouraging new growth and keeping the tree small. Structural pruning, meanwhile, is used to define the tree's basic shape and style. Much of the art of bonsai comes down to the grower's ability to apply pruning techniques so that their tree comes to manifest its desired shape and style.

While indoor bonsai can be maintenance pruned at any time of year, you should ideally wait until the growing season before maintenance pruning your outdoor bonsai. When maintenance pruning your bonsai, start by removing leaves, dead wood, and weeds from the surface of the soil and from the tree itself. Next, trim broken twigs and branches so that the tree can direct its growing energy towards its healthier parts. Remove crossed branches to prevent them from rubbing against each other, to avoid causing wounds that could allow diseases or insects into the tree.

Look for twigs with five or more nodes (joints for leaves to grow out of) and reduce their length to three or four nodes. This encourages new growth while maintaining the small size of the tree. Next, look to the canopy of your tree, and trim shoots and branches that outgrow the intended boundaries of the canopy. This encourages even growth and dense foliage.

Structural pruning involves pruning larger branches to give your tree its intended shape. Place yourself at eye level with the tree and start by removing dead branches. Next, look for branches that don't compliment the intended look of your tree, such as protruding branches, branches with strange twists, branches that cross in front of the trunk, or branches that are otherwise visually unappealing.

Lastly, check the canopy and crown of your tree. Since light must be allowed to reach the tree's lower branches through the canopy, consider whether the foliage needs to be thinned. Remove any suckers (small offshoots often found on the branches or trunk) that detract from the appearance of your tree. Structural pruning should occur during the tree's Winter dormancy to not stunt its growth or cause too much damage.

Making Leaves Smaller

While bonsai is not strictly about the art of creating a miniature version of a full-sized tree, many bonsai growers place emphasis on miniaturing the elements of their tree as much as possible. Making leaves smaller can be an arduous task, but several techniques can be used to achieve this aim.

First—and perhaps most obviously—by choosing a tree species with naturally small leaves, you will find your overall leaf size more in proportion with the rest of your tree. However, some growers purposefully choose larger-leaved varieties as an added challenge.

Remember that bonsai trees grow in the same way as regular full-sized trees—all of which constantly seek sunlight. When trees and plants have insufficient access to sunlight, they tend to increase the size of their leaves as a way of increasing their surface area to let in more light. To counter this tendency, ensure that your trees are receiving sufficient light at all times.

Another technique to reduce your bonsai tree's leaf size is *defoliation*, discussed in the next section.

Defoliation

Defoliation is the practice of removing some of your bonsai tree's foliage to encourage it to grow new leaves, which will usually be smaller and healthier than before. Importantly, some trees cannot withstand defoliation, conifers being one example. Deciduous trees are excellent candidates for selective defoliation as they lose their leaves seasonally anyway. Only ever defoliate a tree that is well-established and healthy.

Defoliation should be carried out only once per year, at the start of Spring when the tree has grown its first leaves of the season. When defoliating, use sterile scissors to remove the leaf at its base. Do not cut off the stem of the leaf—leave that attached to the branch and allow it to fall off on its own.

Surface Roots

Surface roots (also known as nebari) are incredibly important for a bonsai. Not only do they keep the tree securely in its place, but they are also the primary means for the tree to interact with and gain nutrients from the soil. Surface roots are also visually pleasing and are a wonderful addition to many bonsai trees. Surface roots can be created by pruning the downward growing roots regularly, or by using the technique of air layering (discussed later in this chapter).

Trimming surface roots is a stressful event for a bonsai tree and should take place around one year after branch and crown pruning. Any sooner and the health of your tree could suffer irreparably.

Steps for trimming:

1. Gently remove your bonsai from its pot and place it on a working surface.
2. Loosen the roots and soil by softly combing through the roots with your fingers.
3. Locate the primary taproot and remove roots circling the taproot.
4. Identify the thick roots that grow downwards from the primary taproot and remove one-third of their length. Do not remove the hair roots growing outwards from the primary taproot.
5. Lastly, remove about one-third of the lower portion of the roots to create a shallower and more compact root ball.

For trimming/pruning your bonsai, follow these guidelines to encourage your bonsai to grow in a way that suits the overall vision for your tree:

- If your tree features two similar branches at the same height, remove one.
- Remove branches that are too thick compared to other branches.

- Remove branches that are growing vertically or that are misshaped and twisted.
- Remove branches that obscure the trunk or are growing too low.
- Branches towards the bottom of the tree should usually be thicker than those at the top. Remove branches that buck this trend.
- If your tree has a weak area, leave all branches in this area to promote new growth.

Introduction to Air Layering

Air layering—or *toroki* in Japanese—is an advanced technique employed to manipulate root growth. Air layering involves interrupting the existing root system's nutrient stream to force the tree to grow new roots at the desired location. It is an effective method to encourage the growth of surface roots and to reduce the length of your tree's trunk.

There are two primary air layering methods, *tourniquet,* and *ring air layering*. Take note that air layering should only be undertaken during the growing season, typically between early Spring and the first signs of Summer.

The tourniquet method is best for slow-growing trees. To apply the tourniquet method, wrap copper wire around the trunk at the point where you want to encourage the new roots to grow. Doing this will block the nutrient stream and force the growth of new roots. Aim for the wire to cut approximately halfway through the thickness of the bark. You may need to use thicker wire for thicker trunks.

The ring method of air layering involves cutting a ring of bark away from the trunk at the point where you would like to encourage new roots to grow. Cutting the ring will force new roots to grow immediately above in order for the tree to survive. To perform this method, use a sharp blade to cut two parallel slits around the trunk, then remove the bark from between the lines, revealing the underlying hardwood.

Regardless of the air layering technique you've chosen, wrap sphagnum moss around the open wound before wrapping the trunk in plastic. Ensure that the moss is kept moist at all times. Within one to three months, new roots will begin growing out of the moss.

Your tree will be in a state of shock during this time and so should be protected from cold temperatures. Do not make any further changes to the tree until the following Spring, and ideally avoid fertilizing until the next Summer.

Chapter 9: Repotting & Deadwood

Repotting Your Bonsai Tree

The purpose of repotting a bonsai tree is to prevent the roots from becoming root-bound. While repotting won't directly reduce the size of your tree, it does help your tree to continue to survive (and more importantly, thrive!) in a small container. Repotting, combined with root trimming, gives the tree's roots more room to grow while allowing you to replace old bonsai soil with fresh soil.

Some people will be quick to give you hard and fast rules about repotting, such as repotting on a regular schedule of once every one or two years. As with almost every other aspect of growing bonsai trees, these rules should be taken as mere suggestions. Every bonsai is different, and it's impossible to create sweeping generalizations across all tree species. A lot depends on the size of the pot you're using. For example, a fast-growing bonsai in a small pot may need repotting every year, while the same tree in a larger pot could easily thrive for two to three years between needing to be repotted.

Tropical trees can be repotted at any time of year, while other trees generally prefer repotting during Spring when it is first starting to become warm following the end of Winter. Let's look at some of the most common indicators that it is time to repot.

- **Water failing to drain** is a clear sign that it might be time to repot. By now, you will have a good idea of the way the water generally behaves when you water your bonsai—usually by seeping quickly into the soil and draining out the bottom. Once you notice that it is taking longer than usual for the water to drain, it may be time to repot.
- **A change in the time taken for a tree to become dry** can also be a sign that it's time to repot, as the ongoing moistness of the soil can indicate problems with drainage.
- **Hard, compact soil** can make it difficult for water to drain properly.
- **Changes to the root ball** can let you know when it's time to repot. In early Spring, gently remove your tree from its pot and observe the roots to see if they are still contained within the bonsai soil (no need to repot) or whether they have started circling the bottom of the pot (it may be time to consider repotting).
- **A slow rate of growth** compared to previous seasons can indicate several issues. Take the above steps to check if your tree may need repotting.

Before repotting your bonsai, withhold water for a few days to allow the roots to dry somewhat. Ensure you have all the necessary tools and equipment on hand, including a new pot (if necessary), mesh to cover the pot's drain holes, a root rake, pruning scissors, and wire.

First, gently remove the tree from its pot and rake the soil away from the roots using a chopstick or a root rake. If the soil rakes away from the roots easily, your tree can probably handle having all of its soil removed. If the roots have formed a solid root ball but are otherwise healthy, aim to remove the soil from only one side of the root ball. You can remove the soil from the other side during the next repotting.

The next step is to prune some of the roots. Deciduous trees can usually handle having three-quarters of their roots pruned, while evergreens can usually handle having just half of their roots removed. It's always better to be cautious and remove fewer roots than more; otherwise, you could lose your tree.

Now it's time to repot your tree. Ensure that the pot's drainage holes are sufficiently covered with mesh and pass a length of aluminum wire through the drainage holes to secure the tree in place. This will help the tree to establish itself quickly in the new soil. Use 2mm wire for small trees and 3 or 4mm wire for larger trees. Add small amounts of soil to the pot until the tree is standing at its desired height, then secure the tree by twisting the wire. Continue adding soil, using a chopstick to ensure no air bubbles remain.

Thoroughly water your bonsai until the water runs clear, then allow the tree to recover by putting it in a safe position away from direct sunlight for approximately two weeks. Refrain from using fertilizer until you notice new growth emerging.

Deadwood

In the wild, deadwood naturally appears on a tree following an event such as branches snapping due to snow, wind, or ice, or the tree being struck by lightning or exposed to long periods of drought. These events can cause a section of wood to die, with the wound eventually becoming bleached by sunlight.

In the art of bonsai, deadwood can be deliberately created for artistic effect and to mimic the natural phenomena can that affect a tree in the wild. Deadwood is best reserved for evergreen trees, as deciduous trees in the wild tend to lose any deadwood over time. Here are some examples of deadwood.

Jin

A jin is an area of a branch that has been stripped away, mimicking the effects of age, lightning, or strong wind. A jin is created on a bonsai by using jin pliers to strip away lengths of bark from a given start point to the end of the branch, revealing the underlying hardwood. Sharp edges are then sanded away or removed with a concave cutter before the hardwood is bleached with lime sulfur.

Shari

A shari is a vertical section of the tree's trunk without bark. On a bonsai, a shari should be created gradually over several months. Start by removing a narrow strip from the trunk's bark, and slowly widen the strip over the coming months. Use a sharp blade to cut through the bark and jin pliers to tear downwards. Once the ideal shape has been created, use a concave cutter to slightly hollow the trunk, then paint it with lime sulfur.

Uro

An uro is a deep hollow caused by a branch falling off, leaving an indentation. When new wood forms around the area, the hollow appears more pronounced. This effect can be replicated in a bonsai tree by making an irregularly shaped wound in the trunk, or by capitalizing on the removal of an unwanted branch.

10

Chapter 10: Pests, Disease & Seasonal Maintenance

Signs of an Unhealthy Bonsai

As living beings, bonsai trees are susceptible to problems caused by pests and diseases. Part of being a good bonsai hobbyist is understanding your tree and recognizing the signs that its health is declining. This is why it's important to monitor your tree every day and remain vigilant for any of the following symptoms.

- **Drooping** or wilted branches can be an indicator of mineral deficiencies in the soil, poor nutrition, or a mold or mildew infestation.
- **Ragged leaf edges** or leaves that look like they've been bitten most likely have been. The likely cause will be spider mites or aphids.
- **Spots on the leaves** often mean your tree has a fungal infection.
- **Swollen bark** can be a sign of infection underneath the bark, often caused by improper healing following pruning.
- **A tree loose in its pot** shows that the tree's roots are unstable and is often a sign of root rot caused by overwatering or using potting or garden soil instead of bonsai soil.

- **An unexpected loss of foliage** can be a sign of a fungal infection or mold.
- **Wilting or yellowing leaves** can signify a range of issues from overexposure to sunlight, over-or under-watering, or some diseases.

Pests

To reduce the chances of insects and pests setting up home on one or more of your bonsai trees, the most crucial step is to ensure your trees are healthy and well cared for at all times, as insects tend to target unhealthy and vulnerable trees. Also, as much as possible, try to keep your bonsai trees outdoors. Outdoor conditions tend to naturally control many pests.

In addition, try to keep your trees a healthy distance apart from each other to avoid insects jumping from one tree to another. Lastly, keep your work area and tools clean and disinfected to reduce any cross-contamination.

Common Insects and Pests

Aphids appear as colonies of tiny pear-shaped insects and tend to congregate on the undersides and tips of leaves. Look for wilted trees that have stopped growing.

Bag Moths are very adept at replicating the appearance of the bark of a tree. The tiny caterpillars weave small cocoons that can grow to as long as 8cm many months later. It is usually possible to simply pick off the cocoons once you notice them.

Cicadas spend most of their lives living underground, but it is when they emerge into the sunlight that they do their damage. The male cicada emits a call that can be as loud as 90 decibels, while the female lays her eggs in a line along a tiny branch, leaving a scar in the shape of a fishbone. This line of eggs can dramatically weaken the branch, causing it to snap off in a strong wind or when being wired.

Citrus Longhorned Beetles are a Korean beetle but have since been introduced to the United States. The beetles target woody trees and feed on the bark and leaves of bonsai trees.

Fungus Gnats will appear as small grey flies around your tree. The trouble starts when you notice the flies emerging from the soil. Allowing the soil to dry out more than usual can help eradicate these pests.

Mealy Bugs can be difficult to detect and even more challenging to remove. They tend to favor cool and dark areas like in the roots or in thick foliage. Mealy Bugs coat themselves in a waterproof wax, which makes contact sprays all but ineffective. Instead, you'll need to use a systemic spray on your tree to poison the bugs' food supply; however, some trees (such as the Chinese Elm) don't tolerate these sprays.

Mushrooms are not uncommon, especially for trees grown outside, and is actually a sign of healthy soil. Most of the time, mushrooms are not harmful to the tree and can be simply removed using a picking tool such as tweezers.

Passion Vine Hoppers are native to Australia and are also often found on New Zealand's North Island. These pests leave sticky honey-dew that attracts wasps and ants to your trees while causing new growth to be stunted or distorted.

Pine Wilt Nematodes target young shoots and tree sap and sometimes multiply at such a rate that bonsai trees can be destroyed in a single season.

Red Spiders tend to be resistant to pesticides, so it may be worth considering introducing a predatory mite to combat the problem.

Scale insects can be controlled with a mineral oil spray; however, this will only kill live pests and won't affect the eggs. Multiple applications will be required to eradicate this pest.

Snails tend to affect some trees more than others, such as the Fukien Tea, which is also sensitive to pesticides. Instead, try introducing a predator or attempt to manually remove the snails yourself.

Spider Mites appear as small yellow speckles on the surfaces of your leaves, and soon cause your leaves to turn brown and eventually die.

Spruce Spider Mites attack the sap of trees to such an extent that the tree will eventually die. The mites themselves are hard to detect, so look out for yellowed sections of your tree. An insecticide can help combat the problem once identified.

Thrips make their presence known by leaving fine yellow spots on leaves, followed by a metallic sheen.

White Flies appear as white moths that rest on the surfaces of leaves and will flutter up in a cloud when disturbed, only to quickly resettle back on the leaves.

Diseases

A diseased bonsai tree can soon die if not treated properly. It is essential to recognize the symptoms of a bonsai disease (discussed at the start of this chapter) and act fast to resolve the problem after it is first identified.

Some tree species are more likely to become diseased or to pick up a certain type of disease. To avoid disease, it's worthwhile researching your particular species to understand what diseases they might be susceptible to contracting. As always, aim to keep your trees healthy and well cared for, as this reduces the chance of contracting a disease.

First Steps to Take When You Notice Disease

Tree diseases are easily spread not only between trees but also between different parts of a single tree—making it vitally important for you to act fast to contain the threat.

When you first suspect that one of your trees is diseased, immediately isolate the tree away from other trees. Remove all affected areas of the tree and spray the healthy areas with an appropriate fungicide. Properly sterilize all tools used to trim and treat the tree, then check for possible precipitating factors such as overly wet soil or a lack of ventilation. Ensure that the tree is located in a location with appropriate sunlight and airflow to prevent another infection.

Recognizing Common Diseases that Affect Bonsai Trees

Black Spot appears as black patches on leaves and will soon cause the leaves to become yellow and then fall off.

Leaf Spot is a fungus that will appear as grey, brown, black, or white spots on branches or leaves.

Mold/Mildew will appear as a black or white substance in a damp area of your tree with insufficient ventilation and sunlight.

Rust is a fungal infection that appears as brown, red, orange, or yellow raised bumps on the underside of your tree's leaves, causing the leaves to soon curl and fall off.

Chlorosis is the result of a damaged root system and will cause leaves to appear yellow with green veins while the rest of the tree starts to wilt.

Root Rot is the result of overwatering, improper drainage, or the use of the wrong type of soil. It causes waterlogged, brown roots, and stunted growth of the tree.

Canker Diseases are characterized by reduced tree growth, faded leaf colors, and swellings under the bark. Most canker diseases begin shortly after pruning.

Twig and Tip Blight tend to affect Junipers and cause new shoots to die and existing needles to turn brown and fall off.

Powdery Mildew can result when a tree's leaves stay wet overnight after being watered in the evening and presents itself as fine white powder on the leaves.

Weather

Replicating Extreme Weather Conditions For Your Bonsai

The cascade bonsai style was created to replicate the style of some trees in the wild that have been affected by extreme weather or natural conditions such as heavy snowfall, mudslides, or landslides. When a tree encounters these conditions in the wild, it will cause the trunk to twist downwards while the branches grow in an upwards and outwards direction as they search for sunlight. A stunning cascade style bonsai tree is a way of paying homage to the struggles of trees in the wild that will go to any length to survive.

Caring for Your Bonsai During Winter

It is important to remember that bonsai trees—even those grown indoors—are not houseplants. Subject to some exceptions discussed below, bonsai trees should spend sufficient time outdoors and should be exposed to the Winter elements for their survival and longevity.

Normal Winter Conditions

Hardy tree species should be left outdoors during Winter, as they need to experience Winter dormancy as part of their typical annual cycle. Such trees are perfectly adept at preparing themselves for the Winter months by hardening their stems and creating a type of antifreeze by storing sugars. Dormancy begins when temperatures dip below 50 degrees Fahrenheit (10 degrees Celsius). You will need to protect your tree from dehydration, excessive wind, and overwatering from rain and snowfall. This can be achieved by moving your tree to a sheltered outdoor area.

Extreme Winter Conditions

Your tree may need external protection should temperatures drop below 15 degrees Fahrenheit (-9 degrees Celsius). Bring your tree into a protected area where temperatures will remain between 15 to 50 degrees Fahrenheit (-12 to 10 degrees Celsius)—any warmer, and the tree will come out of dormancy. You will typically need to water your bonsai two or three times a week during Winter, but be sure not to go too crazy on the fertilizer.

Winter Care for Tropical and Subtropical Bonsai

Tropical and subtropical bonsai do not experience Winter dormancy and must be sheltered from temperatures below 50 degrees Fahrenheit (10 degrees Celsius) year-round. Use growing lights/greenhouses if adequate sunlight is unavailable, and ensure you maintain your typical watering regime.

11

Chapter 11: Misconceptions & Common Mistakes

How to Avoid Killing Your Bonsai Tree

On your lifelong journey to becoming an experienced bonsai grower, it's possible but not certain that you will kill a few trees along the way. My goal with this book is to reduce the likelihood of that happening.

While some species are relatively tolerant of mistakes, others can be less forgiving. Trees—whether bonsai or in their natural full-sized form—generally don't die of old age. Therefore if your tree dies, you can safely assume it's because you've made one or more mistakes.

Some people estimate that as many as 75% of newly purchased bonsai trees will die in the first month! If you lose a bonsai, know that you're in good company. While it's disappointing to watch your beloved bonsai die, it is most important that you use the experience as a learning opportunity. Work out where you went wrong and learn the lesson, so you don't make the same mistake again.

If your tree is starting to look worse for wear, or you're determined that this tree will be THE ONE that survives long-term, take the following steps to avoid killing your tree.

First, identify your tree. Care guidelines will always vary depending on your tree's species, so the first step is to know the origins of your tree. If you have innocently purchased a tree labeled only as a "bonsai tree," skip forward to Chapter 12 to learn how to properly identify your tree. Bonsai trees are delicate and require specialized care. By understanding the needs of your tree species' full-sized version, you can understand how to apply and adapt those needs to a bonsai.

The most important decision that you'll need to make once you have identified your tree is where it will live. Some bonsai trees need to live outdoors, while others can tolerate either indoor or outdoor placement. Chapter 4 contains information regarding indoor versus outdoor living.

Now that you understand which species of bonsai you have, it's time to learn the correct feeding, watering, and daily sunlight requirements of your tree. Most mistakes that end up killing a tree arise from watering or fertilizing—whether too much or too little. Revisit Chapter 7 and come to a firm understanding of how to correctly feed and water your bonsai. Remember never to water your bonsai on a strict schedule. Instead, learn how to test the bonsai soil for dryness. Over time, you will come to recognize the signs that indicate your bonsai is ready to be watered.

If you are confident that you have placed your bonsai correctly (according to its species and that the feeding and watering regimen is optimal) but your bonsai is showing signs that it may be dying, it's time to consider whether pests or diseases are the culprit. See Chapter 10 for information about common pests and diseases that can wreak havoc on a bonsai tree. Perhaps perform a careful inspection of your bonsai tree's foliage, and gently lift your tree from its pot to check for insects within the root structure.

Mistakes Obtaining and Locating Your Tree

Keeping an Outdoor Tree Indoors

The most common mistake made in the world of bonsai is keeping an outdoor bonsai indoors. For many people, this mistake comes about due to pop culture and media representations of bonsai trees being similar to houseplants—living indoors on an office desk or windowsill. As you know, most bonsai species simply cannot survive indoors and require an outdoor living environment. In the next chapter, you'll find a comprehensive list of bonsai tree species with detailed information on those that can tolerate indoor living and those that must remain outdoors. Keeping an outdoor tree species indoors will slowly cause your tree to die.

Providing Insufficient Sunlight to an Indoor Tree

The majority of bonsai trees which can tolerate indoor living are subtropical species that require plenty of sunlight. A common mistake with indoor bonsai trees is placing them in an inappropriate position where they do not receive adequate sunlight. Indoor bonsai trees must be placed on a windowsill to receive as much sunlight as possible.

If you don't have an appropriate window on which to place your bonsai, you will need to consider acquiring artificial grow lights. Otherwise, your bonsai will begin to shrink due to a lack of photosynthesis and will soon start to wilt and die.

Positioning an Indoor Tree in an Inappropriate Location

In addition to ensuring that your indoor bonsai receives plenty of sunlight through a window, it is equally important to make sure that your bonsai isn't positioned too close to any electrical devices that emit heat, such as televisions, microwaves, washers and dryers, heating and cooling systems, and computers. These electrical devices create a dry environment and interfere with the proper ventilation otherwise required by indoor bonsai trees.

Placing Your Outdoor Tree in an Insect-Prone Area

Bonsai trees are prone to becoming infested with insects or affected by disease. While there are ways of treating a bonsai after it has become infested, such treatments are pointless if your bonsai is placed in an area where it is likely to again become infested. If the area is one that is often plagued with insects or where similar trees continue to suffer from infestation, you'll need to find a new location for your bonsai tree.

Positioning an Outdoor Bonsai in a Poor Location

Not all outdoor bonsai trees will have the same requirements when it comes to sunlight. Some trees will need as much sunlight as possible, while others will prefer afternoon shade or partial shade at all times. A common bonsai mistake is to assume that all outdoor trees have the same sunlight preferences.

Collecting a Wild Tree Without Knowing its Species

Care must be taken when collecting a tree from the wild. A common mistake in this area is collecting a tree without knowing its species. Before collecting a tree, take photos of it and properly identify the tree, then ensure that you have the right location to position the tree at home, either indoors or outdoors. Then revisit the location to collect the tree once you have satisfied yourself that you will be able to meet its needs.

Collecting a Wild Tree Without the Proper Tools

A related common mistake when collecting a tree from the wild is to take it the first time you see it, even if you are confident that you can identify its species. Collecting a tree from the wild should be a mindful experience. Wait until you have your bonsai tools with you and ensure you have prepared a place at home for your new bonsai before collecting it from the wild.

Purchasing a Tree Without Knowing its Species

When purchasing a bonsai tree or a pre-bonsai, ensure that the tree species is clearly identified. A tree simply labeled as a "bonsai tree" without any other identifying information is not a true bonsai. Such selling practices are a clear warning that the seller is not experienced with bonsai growing and will not be a good source of information about your particular species of tree.

Tooling Mistakes

Buying Too Many Tools in the Beginning

It can be exciting getting started with a new hobby and bonsai growing is no exception. A common mistake beginner bonsai growers make is buying a complete set of bonsai tools from the outset. Not only can this be a costly exercise but it is usually overkill.

It is better to start with the few tools you need to begin your bonsai journey (including standard bonsai shears, concave pruners, wire cutters, and chopsticks) and purchase new tools (and upgrade your existing tools) as the need arises. You will learn so much about bonsai as the years go by, so waiting to purchase the right tools as you need them will ensure you make the best buying decisions at the appropriate time.

Using Garden Shears Instead of Pruning Shears

Pruning shears are arguably the most important tool you'll need when growing a bonsai. To avoid needlessly harming or scarring your tree, it is best to start with proper bonsai pruning shears rather than using common gardening shears or secateurs. If you only buy one bonsai tool at the start of your journey, make it a proper pair of bonsai shears.

Removing Branches with Anything Other Than Concave Branch Cutters

When it comes time to remove full branches from your bonsai, it will become necessary to invest in a pair of concave branch cutters. These branch cutters leave a concave wound, which will heal faster and with less chance of scarring than a flat wound. Concave cutters will also give you greater control over the tool, allowing you to cut thicker branches and knobs than with a flat tool.

Planting, Soil, Fertilizing, and Watering Mistakes

Underwatering

In the wild, trees use their extensive root system to dig deep into the ground in search of water and nutrients. Bonsai trees, on the other hand, spend their entire existence contained in small pots. Their ability to find water on their own is extremely limited, making it vitally important that you provide them with the right amount of water as needed.

While some bonsai trees are relatively hardy and can withstand short periods of drought, the majority of bonsai trees will soon die if deprived of water. When a bonsai tree's soil becomes dry, its roots dry out, and its foliage shows signs of dehydration. A deciduous tree will tend to lose its leaves, while the foliage of an evergreen tree may change color and lose its vitality if not watered enough.

Overwatering

When a bonsai tree dies, it is usually because of issues with watering or fertilizing. Among these issues, overwatering is the most common way to kill your bonsai tree. Overwatering tends to occur either because the tree is being watered too frequently or because incorrect soil is being used (i.e., common gardening or potting mix instead of bonsai soil), which retains water and keeps the roots wet. Wet roots will soon cause root rot—a sure-fire way to kill your bonsai tree.

Lack of Fertilizer

Fertilizer is tree food, and just as humans cannot survive for long without food, trees similarly cannot survive without proper fertilization. In the wild, trees use their root system to search for nutrients under the ground. When confined to a bonsai pot, a bonsai tree relies on you to provide it with the nutrients it needs to survive. Without fertilization, a bonsai will soon grow weak and will eventually die.

Failing to Recognize Toxins in Your Bonsai Soil

Toxic soil is a relatively common bonsai problem yet is often not properly understood by beginners. If you notice your bonsai tree's foliage turning an unusual color or otherwise appearing unhealthy, you should first rule out any problems with watering or fertilizing.

The next step to take is to conduct a soil test. If the soil contains harmful toxins, you will need to flush them out using generous amounts of water or consider starting fresh with new soil by repotting your bonsai. Avoid fertilizing until your bonsai has recovered from its repotting and has returned to its former state of strong vitality.

Too Much Fertilizer

When humans are unwell, they will often reframe from eating food to give their bodies a chance to heal. Similarly, bonsai trees should not be over-fertilized when they are in the process of healing from a traumatic event such as repotting, during periods of extreme heat, or when recovering from a pest infestation or disease. Additionally, humans do not eat while sleeping. For bonsai trees, sleeping is equivalent to Winter dormancy. Refrain from feeding your bonsai during Winter—a time when your bonsai is not growing and is simply lying dormant until Spring.

Mistakes When Styling, Shaping, Wiring, and Pruning

Reshaping Too Often

While it can be tempting to make ongoing changes to your bonsai year-round, reshaping too often is a common mistake that can cause a great deal of stress to your tree. At the most, bonsai trees can only tolerate major changes such as redesigning, rewiring, or repotting once a year. More frequent changes will put your bonsai under long-term stress and affect its ability to grow.

Cutting Your Bonsai Tree's Tips

When you feel that your bonsai tree's branches or foliage are growing too long, it can be tempting to simply cut off the tip to shorten their length. However, many tree species (such as Junipers) rely on the tips of their foliage for strength and energy. Removing the tips can dramatically weaken your tree. Instead, follow the tip back until you reach a crotch or fork in the branch, then trim the longer foliage there.

Repotting Mistakes

Repotting Too Often

While repotting is essential to the ongoing health and vitality of your bonsai, repotting too often is a common bonsai mistake—putting unnecessary strain on your tree. Instead, your tree needs time to fully recover anytime it is repotted.

Not Avoiding Air Pockets

Air pocket formations are a common occurrence when repotting a bonsai tree and are as easy to miss as they are to avoid. Air pockets occur when bonsai soil is added around the sides of your tree but not underneath the roots.

To prevent this from occurring, use a bamboo chopstick or a similar simple tool to poke at an angle under the roots when repotting to ensure that the soil fills in the entire space underneath the roots. Otherwise, the roots will be surrounded by soil but will sit directly on a pocket of air, giving them no way to access the vital water and nutrients they desperately need.

Fertilizing Too Soon After Repotting

Repotting causes a great deal of stress to a bonsai tree, and your tree needs sufficient time to recover afterward. Resist the temptation to fertilize your tree immediately after you have finished repotting. Instead, allow your tree a few weeks to re-establish itself in its new soil before you begin feeding it again. Fertilizer should only be given to healthy, stable, and unstressed trees.

Problems With Displaying and Other Ongoing Mistakes

Lack of Patience

Patience can be a difficult skill to master. When starting as a bonsai grower, it can be tempting to be overly enthusiastic and make regular changes to your tree. Sitting back and watching your tree grow without touching it can be almost impossible, especially when you are first getting started. Just as humans need time to recover from an illness or operation, bonsai trees need time to readjust and become resettled after a major change such as being repotted, restyled, or wired.

Bonsai trees grow slowly, and this can be hard for beginner bonsai enthusiasts to grasp and accept. To fulfill your desire to be involved, it can help to have several bonsai tree projects to work on at the same time. While one tree may need time to rest, another may be ready for repotting or reshaping.

Failing to Rotate Your Bonsai

All sides of your bonsai tree need to receive adequate sunlight exposure. A common mistake with both indoor and outdoor bonsai trees is to place them in a well-lit position but then fail to rotate them regularly. This would mean that while you will get to view the "front" or "best" side of the bonsai at all times, not all sides are receiving sufficient levels of sunlight. Remember that the well-being of your bonsai tree must always be your number one priority.

Cutting Corners and Experimenting Too Much

Bonsai masters generally agree that bonsai growing involves a high degree of risk-taking and experimentation. However, a common mistake is to experiment with the basics rather than follow well-known advice. For instance, if a certain tree species must be grown outdoors, experimenting with placing it indoors on a windowsill is a sure-fire way of killing your tree. Similarly, experimenting with using common garden soil or potting mix instead of bonsai soil will almost certainly lead to root rot. A rule of thumb is to first concentrate on mastering what others have perfected before you begin running experiments of your own.

Common Misconceptions About Bonsai

Any tree in a Japanese bonsai pot can be considered a bonsai.

Truth: Bonsai pots are important but are always secondary to the tree itself. A stick in an expensive Japanese bonsai pot is still a stick!

You can buy bonsai seeds that will grow miniature trees.

Truth: There is no such thing as bonsai seeds. Bonsai trees grow from the same seeds as full-sized versions of the same tree. Beware of any bonsai supplier claiming to sell "bonsai seeds".

Bonsais must be constantly pruned.

Truth: The ideal pruning schedule for a particular bonsai will depend on the type of tree and its typical rate of growth, plus the environment in which it is being grown.

Creating a bonsai tree is cruel.

Truth: It may seem cruel to keep a typically wild tree in a small container, but in reality, bonsai trees only survive when adequately fed, watered, trimmed, and cared for. It is not the size of a bonsai pot that restricts its growth but rather the shaping and maintenance applied to the tree that keeps it small. The majority of bonsai trees are very well cared for and cherished by their artful creators. With the proper attention and dedication, bonsais thrive as much as their full-sized equivalents.

Creating a bonsai tree is difficult.

Truth: Creating and maintaining a bonsai is no more difficult than any other form of gardening. Bonsai growing can seem difficult for some people because of the artistic side of the craft. Keeping a bonsai alive is technically no more difficult than keeping any other type of tree, plant, or shrub alive. However, it is the artistic aspects of bonsai growing such as shaping, wiring, and leaf reducing that people spend the most amount of their time and energy on.

Avoid watering or feeding your bonsai to help stunt its growth.

Truth: Fertilizer is essentially plant food, and it (along with water) is an essential element of keeping a bonsai alive. If a bonsai tree's soil dries out, the root ball will soon stop carrying moisture to the tree, causing the tree to die. Similarly, the small growing container of a bonsai means that the tree does not have access to the same soil nutrients as full-sized trees in the wild. By adding fertilizer to the bonsai soil, you provide the nutrients that would otherwise have been accessible to the tree. This myth generally originates from the mistaken belief that bonsai trees should be encouraged to grow as slowly as possible to stunt their growth. Withholding food or water from your bonsai is an easy way to kill your tree. Learn more about fertilizing and water in Chapter 7.

Bonsai trees are genetically modified dwarf varieties.

Truth: While there are scientific ways to genetically modify the DNA of trees to create dwarf varieties, the art of bonsai is entirely distinct. Bonsai trees are genetically identical to their full-sized counterparts and would grow to full size if special horticultural techniques such as pruning, shaping, and root reduction were not applied.

A bonsai tree will eventually stop growing.

Truth: Like all trees, bonsais will continue to grow throughout their lifespan. If bonsai horticultural techniques were no longer applied and the tree was planted in the wild, the bonsai would eventually grow to full size. Bonsai trees retain their small size through the ongoing application of artistic bonsai growing techniques.

Creating and maintaining bonsai is expensive.

Truth: Many hundreds of years ago, the art of bonsai was reserved for the upper echelons of Chinese society. Since then, bonsai has retained its position as a status symbol for wealthy, elite, or spiritual people. Those who practice bonsai today tend to hold the art in high regard, giving it a perceived high value as a status symbol.

In reality, though, growing a bonsai tree does not have to be an expensive pursuit. It is possible to find inexpensive or second-hand tools that can perform their duties just as well as high-end Japanese tools, and there is no need for an expensive Japanese bonsai pot when you're first getting started. The value of bonsai comes from the time, effort, and care expended in the creation of these splendid trees.

A bonsai will eventually achieve a finished state.

Truth: Should you ever feel that your bonsai is finished and stop pruning, training, and repotting it, you will soon discover that your tree will continue to grow and will quickly become rootbound in its pot or reach the full size that it would otherwise have reached in the wild. Bonsais are a constant work-in-progress and require ongoing maintenance for their entire lifespan.

Fruit on bonsai trees will be miniature versions of full-sized fruit.

Truth: Your bonsai may resemble a miniature version of a full-sized tree, yet it will still bear typical, full-sized fruit. This is because bonsai trees have not been genetically modified and are genetically identical to their full-sized counterparts. Fruit borne on a bonsai tree will grow to standard size and will taste just the same. Keep in mind that fruit grown for the produce section of a supermarket has been specifically grown to be large and without defects, making supermarket fruit generally larger than the equivalent fruit grown in the wild. Fruit grown on your bonsai trees won't be as large as supermarket fruit but will resemble fruits in their most natural form.

Bonsais are planted in regular potting or garden soil.

Truth: Despite bonsai soil being referred to as "soil," it typically contains no real organic matter. Instead, bonsais are grown in a specially formulated mixture that provides just the right combination of air, space, and drainage to cater to bonsai trees' unique needs. Refer to Chapter 6 for more information on bonsai soil.

Bonsais are indoor potted plants.

Truth: In almost every media and pop culture representation of bonsai trees, they are depicted as indoor potted plants. In reality, most bonsais require an outdoor environment with plenty of sunlight to thrive. While some bonsai trees can survive perfectly well indoors, most species need to live outdoors to replicate their natural growing conditions in the wild. Chapters 3 and 4 contain more information about growing bonsais indoors and outdoors.

Leaves on bonsai trees are miniature versions of full-sized leaves.

Truth: Bonsai trees are genetically identical to full-sized trees, and it is only through specific horticultural practices that the roots, trunk, and branches of a tree can be reduced to create the bonsai art form. Similarly, special techniques must be applied to reduce the tree's leaf size if desired. Find out more about these techniques in Chapter 8.

Only imported plants can be true bonsais.

Truth: While it is possible to import a bonsai tree, most bonsais are created using local plants or trees that are native to your area. For a bonsai tree to flourish, you must be able to replicate the conditions the tree would have been exposed to in the wild. A species native to an area with a dramatically different climate will struggle to thrive under different conditions.

Bonsais must be under 12 inches in height.

Truth: No mention is made of bonsai trees being restricted to a certain size or height. While there are different size classes in official bonsai competitions, any tree that is planted in a container and which conforms to bonsai styles and standards can be considered a true bonsai.

The aim of growing bonsai is to make the tree look as old as possible.

Truth: In some instances, specific tree species are selected to create a bonsai due to the propensity for that tree to appear older than it actually is. While there is certainly beauty to be found in a bonsai that resembles a miniature version of an ancient tree, there is nothing to say that an older-looking bonsai is inherently better or more valuable than a bonsai with a younger appearance.

Only trees can be turned into bonsai.

Truth: While bonsais are often generically referred to as "bonsai trees", there are plenty of plant and shrub varieties that lend themselves perfectly to the art of bonsai. For example, shrubs like Azaleas and

Cotoneasters are popular bonsai species, and even a common Grapevine can be trained in bonsai form and still produce edible fruits. See the extensive list of popular bonsai species in Chapter 12 for more information.

Bonsai is its own tree species.

Truth: The term "bonsai tree" refers to the style, placement, and growing conditions applied to the tree and does not refer to a particular tree species. This myth comes from the mistaken assumption that equates "bonsai tree" with a tree species like Apple trees or Elm trees.

Pruning the roots of a bonsai eventually kills the tree.

Truth: Root pruning does not harm a bonsai. Bonsai growers take much pride and care in their trees and would not continue to engage in a practice that would eventually kill their tree. The effect of root pruning is quite the opposite—it benefits the tree by removing dying roots and promoting strong, new roots.

The purpose of repotting a bonsai is to put the tree in a larger pot.

Truth: While there are some instances when a bonsai tree will be repotted into a larger pot because it is outgrowing its current pot, most of the time, bonsai trees are potted back into the same container. Repotting—discussed in detail in Chapter 9—involves raking the roots, removing some of the root mass, and allowing for improved aeration and drainage, which is necessary to keep the tree healthy.

Small bonsais are less valuable than large bonsais (or vice versa).

Truth: The value of a bonsai always comes down to the quality of the tree and the amount of time, care, and effort that has been expended on its growth. Sometimes this will mean a large bonsai fetching a high price, while other times, a tiny bonsai will be the most valuable one in a bonsai collection. No set rule equates a bonsai tree's size with its value.

12

Chapter 12: Profiles of Bonsai Species

There is no singular correct way of delineating how many bonsai tree species currently exist. Much depends on how we define bonsai and on the new and unique ways that growers can apply bonsai horticultural techniques to turn regular tree species into works of art. According to the Magiminiland website[1], there are 150 tree families containing 1,744 individual tree species capable of being grown as bonsai trees. This figure, though, does not take into account hybrid tree species.

Additionally, while all of the 1,744 species in the Magiminiland list may be capable of being grown as a bonsai, not all are well-suited to the art. Below you will find a comprehensive list of the most common and popular bonsai species today. These tree species are considered popular for being either low-maintenance, easy to care for, able to grow indoors, or for specific aesthetic reasons that make them ideal for the art of bonsai, such as having naturally small foliage or an attractive bark or trunk structure.

How to Identify Your Bonsai

If you are growing a bonsai and are unsure of your tree's species—or you have identified a potentially viable pre-bonsai or sapling in a nursery and want to know more about its requirements—there are several ways to identify your tree. The Bonsai Empire website[2] includes an especially useful bonsai identification tool that will allow you to narrow down your tree's potential species by identifying trademark characteristics, beginning with its foliage.

Alternatively, try taking advantage of the combined knowledge found in a bonsai social media group, chat room, or message board by posting photos of your tree and asking for help identifying it. You can also try taking your tree to a local bonsai club or reputable nursery for advice.

Common & Popular Bonsai Species

Acacia (Wattle)

A genus encompassing over 1,200 species, many Acacia varieties are suitable for the art of bonsai. These evergreen, broadleaf shrubs and trees require ample sunlight but will resist direct sunlight. Their ideal location is indoors near a well-positioned window. Acacia bonsai require daily watering but avoid overwatering them on each occasion.

Adenium (Desert Rose)

With its glossy leaves, vibrant colored flowers, bulbous base, and thick trunk, the Adenium has all the characteristics of a stunning bonsai. Renowned for its fast growth and natural appearance, this succulent tree is native to Arabia and Africa and makes an ideal bonsai for beginners. Choose a sunny location with sufficient wind shelter. Unless you live in a tropical climate, you will need to bring your bonsai indoors during Winter and maintain a temperature of approximately 50 degrees Fahrenheit (10 degrees Celsius). Under favorable growing conditions, your Adenium bonsai will reward you with large red, pink, or white flowers.

Apple

While Apple trees can be grown indoors, they prefer an outdoor environment under direct sunlight. Native to the tropics in America,

Apple trees feature dark green leaves and can be cultivated into various bonsai styles. Producing pink and white flowers during the Summer, a well-cared Apple tree will replace its flowers with apple fruit.

Azalea (Rhododendron)

The Azalea shrub has specific growing requirements—including regular care, acidic soil, specific fertilizer, and water free of lime—and as such is not known as a particularly beginner-friendly bonsai choice. Bonsai growers who choose to tackle an Azalea will need to be on the lookout for insects and pests and must protect their specimens from frost. Those who can cope with the Azalea's challenging nature will be rewarded with attractive flowers and a stunning bonsai structure.

Bahama Berry

Even in their first few years, a Bahama Berry bonsai will appear deceptively (and most would agree attractively) old thanks to its long bark and twisted, slim trunk. Borne from tropical climates, the Bahama Berry tree requires full sun exposure year-round. Despite being high maintenance, this tree is a favorite with more experienced bonsai growers.

Bald Cypress

The Bald Cypress is native to Central America and southern parts of the United States. As a deciduous tree, the Bald Cypress loses its soft, light green leaves during Winter. Strictly an outdoor bonsai, the Bald Cypress requires daily watering and full sun—but will also need protection from extreme frost.

Bamboo

Bamboo trees are incredibly hard to apply bonsai techniques to, leaving these intriguing trees to the most experienced bonsai artists.

Baobab

The Baobab is a slow-growing tree that will eventually develop a deeply furrowed, bottle-shaped trunk. Native to Africa, the Baobab requires a warm climate and is considered easy to care for.

Bird Plum

A native Asian tree or shrub, the Bird Plum features small white flowers that later bear sweet black fruits. Its leaves are small and shiny, and its bark is an attractive dark brown, giving the Bird Plum the perfect appearance for the art of bonsai. While the Bird Plum performs the best living outdoors, they do require a shady environment and must be sheltered from frost.

Black Olive

Unlike the regular Olive tree, the Black Olive produces fruits that are not edible for humans. As a delicate bonsai, the Black Olive features a multitude of branches layered with spines. In the wild, these trees tend to grow in warm areas near the sea, making their bonsai equivalent highly tolerant of heat and salty conditions.

Bodhi (Ficus Religiosa)

The Bodhi is a hardy, fast-growing tropical tree that thrives in warm environments and requires protection from frost and cold conditions. Its shiny, heart-shaped leaves initially appear bronze and later turn into a glossy green as the tree matures. Bonsai growers wishing to practice the art of leaf size reduction will find the Bodhi an excellent tree with which to experiment.

Bougainvillea

The Bougainvillea is a stunning tree that makes an equally attractive bonsai. Its trademark papery blossoms (which are its leaves rather than its flowers) make a beautiful display on this fast-growing tree. The Bougainvillea requires at least five hours of sunlight every day and must be protected from frost. Those wishing to experiment with different types of bonsai styles will find the Bougainvillea a willing subject for almost all styles, except for formal upright.

Boxwood

Despite being most commonly thought of as a hedging plant, the Boxwood can also be styled into an attractive bonsai with its light beige bark and bright green leaves. In the wild, the Boxwood grows under the canopy of larger trees, so its bonsai form will grow best when placed outdoors in partial shade. While the Boxwood needs protection from extreme frost, it is an otherwise hardy outdoor bonsai. The Boxwood is tolerant of shaping with wire and even aggressive pruning, making it an excellent species for beginner bonsai enthusiasts looking to experiment with wiring, shaping, and pruning.

Brazilian Rain

As its name suggests, the Brazilian Rain is native to the rainforests of Brazil. With compound leaves that close at night and open during the day, the Brazilian Rain is easy to care for and ideally suited for growing inside your home.

Bromeliad

With an intense need for plenty of sunlight, the Bromeliad requires an outdoor setting and plenty of moisture. However, make sure not to overwater your Bromeliad each time, as being waterlogged will cause a lack of air in the root system, causing suffocation. Despite requiring specific growing conditions, the Bromeliad is surprisingly durable thanks in part to its delicate and complicated root system. Leaf colors can range dramatically, from gold and green to shades of red and maroon.

Brush Cherry

Suitable for indoor or outdoor positioning, the Brush Cherry will reward your patient handling with pretty white flowers that later bear red fruits. With glossy green leaves, this evergreen shrub needs plenty of water year-round.

Buddha's Ear

A native to Southeast Asia, as the name might suggest, the Buddha's Ear can thrive in either indoor or outdoor growing conditions. Their heart-shaped leaves are charmingly glossy and are perfectly complemented by their tiny flowers, which produce miniature berries. The Buddha's Ear grows only a few leaves at a time—a feature that makes the Buddha's Ear a unique bonsai choice.

Buddhist Pine

A predominantly indoor bonsai, the Buddhist Pine requires ongoing damp soil and a warm growing climate. This tropical tree features large needle-shaped dark green leaves and must be protected from frost.

Buttonwood

The Buttonwood is often dismissed as a bonsai species due to its perceived lack of attractiveness compared with other more popular tree species. However, the Buttonwood is an excellent starter bonsai for beginners and can be highly rewarding. For best results, place your Buttonwood outdoors under direct sunlight and make sure to water it regularly.

Cactus Combo

While not all Cactus plants are suitable for bonsai planting, those that do not naturally grow taller than 10 inches can be forged into an attractive cactus combination. Whilst not a true bonsai in the strict sense, a grouping of specially chosen cactus plants in a bonsai pot can perfectly complement an existing bonsai display.

Cape Honeysuckle

Many bonsai enthusiasts have taken on the Cape Honeysuckle as a bonsai project, lured in by the plant's beautiful colored flowers. However, the Cape Honeysuckle can be tricky to sustain and has very particular growing requirements. With an intense need for direct sunlight, the Cape Honeysuckle needs to stay outdoors and is not considered an easy choice for beginners.

Cedar

The Cedar is an impressive evergreen conifer with rugged bark that can be manipulated into a multitude of bonsai styles. This pine species require direct sun but not too much water, preferring instead for its soil to become partially dry between watering. With a need for close attention, the Cedar is better suited for experienced bonsai growers.

Celtis

The Celtis needs an outdoor growing environment but won't perform well in full sunlight. Choose a consistently shaded outdoor area and ensure that your Celtis's soil remains damp at all times.

Cherry Blossom

While native to and commonly found throughout Asia, the Cherry Blossom is most commonly associated with Japan. Its stunning flowers can be a sight to behold, leading many bonsai enthusiasts to tackle a Cherry Blossom as a bonsai project. Your Cherry Blossom will need protection from intense sunlight, particularly during Winter.

Chinese Elm

As another native to eastern parts of Asia, the Chinese Elm is highly tolerant to styling and pruning and tends to easily recover from mistakes. This robust tree prefers an indoor environment with morning and evening sunlight. With a twisting trunk offset by a multitude of tiny leaves, the Chinese Elm has high water absorption rates and requires regular watering.

Chinese Juniper

The Chinese Juniper is a popular bonsai species for beginners and experienced growers alike, thanks in part to its inherently twisted or bent truck and its propensity to acquire deadwood in older age. The Chinese Juniper is easy to grow, provided you're not tempted to water it too often or too heavily. The Chinese Juniper's leaf texture can vary from fine to coarse, with its leaf color ranging between light and dark green, sometimes with a blue tinge.

Chinese Pepper (Szechuan Pepper)

A predominantly indoor bonsai, the Chinese Pepper must be protected from frost and temperatures lower than 50 degrees Fahrenheit (10 degrees Celsius). The Chinese Pepper requires almost continuous watering, especially during periods of high growth. A subtropical tree, the Chinese Pepper's small leaves make them an ideal species for the art of bonsai.

Chinese Quince

The Chinese Quince is not suited for those looking to grow the tiniest of bonsai trees, as it produces naturally large leaves and egg-shaped, large yellow fruits. For those content with a larger bonsai, the Chinese Quince can be resilient and easy to care for—provided it is protected in Winter.

Citrus (Lemon or Orange)

As subtropical trees, Citrus bonsai trees need plenty of water, particularly during the hottest months. When grown under the right conditions, Citrus trees will produce sweet-smelling white flowers followed by citrus fruits.

Common Beech

The Common Beech is a slow-growing tree that makes an attractive medium for large-sized bonsai tree growing. Perfectly suited to an upright bonsai style, the Common Beech prefers either full sun or partial shade but must be shaded from intense afternoon sunlight. The Common Beech is tolerant of heavy pruning practices and grows pleasingly small leaves.

Common Juniper

Despite its name, the Common Juniper is a protected species and must not be collected from the wild. When sourced from a reputable nursery, the Common Juniper makes an ideal bonsai species due to its small and sharp yet soft leaves.

Corean Hornbeam

With stunning yellow and red hues during the Fall months, the Corean Hornbeam's naturally knobby trunk and small leaves make it an ideal choice for a bonsai project.

Cotoneaster

The Cotoneaster is a deciduous shrub that prefers growing outdoors in direct sunlight. A native Chinese shrub, the Cotoneaster naturally lends itself to the cascade style or—for more adventurous bonsai growers—can be planted on a rock. The Cotoneaster's leaves change color from one season to the next, ranging from red, pink, and white in Spring and leading to red berries in the Fall. If you wire your Cotoneaster, do so in the Spring before blossoming begins.

Crabapple

The Crabapple is a robust tree that can be cultivated into a pleasingly small bonsai project. With pretty flowers that bear either red or yellow fruit, the Crabapple requires high levels of water and sunlight.

As a hands-on tree, you'll need to stay vigilant to ensure diseases or pests don't take over.

Crepe Myrtle

The Crepe Myrtle is a deciduous subtropical tree that is native to both Australia and parts of Asia. With its naturally unique branch structure and purple, white, or pink flowers, the Crepe Myrtle makes for an attractive bonsai tree. As the Crepe Myrtle sheds its bark, you'll notice beautiful brown, grey, and sometimes pink under-bark.

Dawn Redwood

A Chinese tree, the Dawn Redwood features opposite leaves (see Chapter 3) and must not be overwatered. Intolerant to frost, the Dawn Redwood must be brought indoors during cold spells or otherwise protected from frigid temperatures.

Desert Rose

The Desert Rose is not strictly a bonsai tree but is often considered to be an honorary member of this exclusive club due to its ability to be grown successfully in a small pot. The Desert Rose should live outdoors during the warmer months and receive protection indoors during the Winter.

Dogwood

The Dogwood tree features deep green vegetation that changes color to shades of red and purple during the Fall, followed by the production of an impressive white flower towards the end of Spring. Preferring shady locations, the Dogwood requires plenty of free air and tolerates pruning and wire training easily.

Duranta

The Duranta is a tropical tree with unusual thorns offset by bright blue flowers and light green leaves. The Duranta's fruits are poisonous to humans but are a favorite with wild doves. With a need for plenty of sunshine, the Duranta is intolerant to frost.

Dwarf Jade

The Dwarf Jade is a semi-evergreen soft-wooded tree or shrub native to Africa and requires warm conditions, as well as plenty of sunlight and protection from frost. However, its water requirements are minimal. With its small, shiny, thick leaves and thick trunks, the Dwarf Jade makes an attractive bonsai and is an excellent choice for beginners.

Dwarf Pomegranate

The Dwarf Pomegranate is not an easy bonsai to grow but can be well worth the effort when it produces its trademark large red flower and attracts a variety of insects. The Dwarf Pomegranate requires ongoing care and high levels of water, sunshine, and air circulation.

Dwarf Schefflera

The Dwarf Schefflera is one of the more popular indoor bonsai species, as it is easy to train and forms aerial roots. As a drought-resistant variety, the Dwarf Schefflera is highly sought after by beginner and experienced bonsai enthusiasts alike, especially as it is tolerant of mistakes and hard to kill. While the Dwarf Schefflera prefers indirect bright light, it can survive just as well in lesser lighting conditions. For those looking to experiment with the banyan bonsai style, the Dwarf Schefflera is an ideal starting point.

European Larch

The European Larch is easy to care for as it tolerates frost reasonably well and loves sunlight. A native to the mountains of Europe, the European Larch grows clusters of needles and long shoots that are both soft and flexible. The European Larch loses its leaves in the Fall.

European Yew

The European Yew is a contradiction as it is part of the conifer family yet bears no cones. A popular choice for hedges, the European Yew can be easily styled as a small bonsai tree or shrub. With dark green leaves and bright red fruit, the European Yew continues to surprise as one of only a few conifers that can thrive in the shade. Its sensitive roots necessitate protection from frost during Winter.

Ficus

The Ficus is a genus of more than 850 species, most of which have smooth grey bark and shiny green leaves. These evergreen trees require plenty of light but can be successfully grown indoors or outdoors under the right lighting conditions. Ficus trees are easy to style and make mistakes or even occasional carelessness in their stride, making the Ficus a perfect first project for beginner bonsai growers or those looking to experiment with different styles.

Firethorn

The Firethorn is a genus with ten species, many of which lend themselves perfectly to the art of bonsai. With high water demands during Winter, the Firethorn will reward growers with plenty of dark foliage and small red fruit. The Firethorn is native to Asia and the Mediterranean and prefers temperate climates.

Flame Tree

With large golden or red flowers, the Flame Tree blossoms spectacularly between Spring and Winter. The Flame Tree is a tropical species of tree that is interestingly technically part of the legume family.

Flowering Apricot

The Flowering Apricot is synonymous with Spring in Japan and makes a stunning bonsai specimen. As a leafless tree with a gnarled, black trunk, the Flowering Apricot produces striking red, pink, or white flowers. Not suited for bonsai beginners, the Flowering Apricot can be difficult to style and prune, as its branches and twigs are brittle and prone to snapping or dying.

Fuchsia

Fuchsia trees have specific growing requirements, including frost protection, an outdoor environment, regular pruning, and plenty of water. In return, your Fuchsia bonsai will provide large and brightly colored flowers in Spring time.

Fukien Tea (Carmona)

The Fukien Tea is native to Australia and south-eastern parts of Asia and can be successfully grown either indoors or outdoors, preferring temperatures between 50 and 75 degrees Fahrenheit (10 to 24 degrees Celsius). The Fukien Tea is considered a difficult bonsai to grow, but your efforts will be well rewarded when you see your tree's naturally small and shiny, dark green leaves and its year-round tiny white flowers and occasional red berries, offset by its brown or grey bark. Maintaining your Fukien Tea bonsai requires specialized skills and plenty of experience, making this species one for beginner bonsai growers to work towards.

Gardenia

The Gardenia is an evergreen shrub native to subtropical areas and can develop strongly scented white flowers. If allowed to pollinate, the flowers will later bear interesting orange fruits.

Ginkgo

The Gingko is a deciduous tree with fan-shaped leaves and is native to China. Interestingly, the Gingko is thought to date back more than 270 million years, giving it the honor of being known as a living fossil! Requiring moist soil and outdoor growing conditions, the Gingko is sometimes able to grow on a rock and will lose its yellow leaves in Winter.

Ginseng Ficus

The Ginseng Ficus is commonly regarded as an excellent bonsai choice for beginners, due to its hardy and forgiving nature. This evergreen broadleaf tree naturally grows interesting-looking twisting aerial roots and dark green leaves, which are typically oval-shaped. With a preference for indirect light and a warm growing environment, the Ginseng Ficus grows well indoors with moist soil.

Grapevine

When grown in the wild, Grapevines are climbing vines that produce edible grapes. In its bonsai form, the Grapevine becomes a tree or shrub but can continue to produce edible fruit. The Grapevine prefers to grow outdoors in a warm environment and can be fairly picky about its growing conditions. Nurturing a Grapevine bonsai is best left to more experienced growers with plenty of time to dedicate to the Grapevine's sometimes daily care requirements.

Green Mound Juniper

The Green Mound Juniper is a popular choice for those just starting with bonsai, as it is easy to maintain and tolerant of regular trimming.

Resilient in many types of climates, the Green Mound Juniper prefers living outdoors but needs protection against direct sunlight. For bonsai growers looking to experiment with different bonsai styles, the Green Mound Juniper (with its small leaves and resilient nature) is an excellent choice.

Guava

Suitable for several different bonsai styles, including formal and informal upright, broom, semi-cascade, and slanting, the Guava tree is an easy-to-maintain bonsai that produces impressive-looking fruits under the right conditions. Your Guava tree prefers a sunny outdoor location for most of the year but should be brought inside or otherwise protected in Winter.

Hawaiian Umbrella

The Hawaiian Umbrella is a natural first bonsai for beginners due to its low maintenance demands and suitability for indoor living. Preferring low humidity and dim lighting, the Hawaiian Umbrella features compound leaves and makes a lovely starter bonsai.

Hibiscus

The Hibiscus requires ongoing sun exposure and frequent watering, making it a relatively high-maintenance bonsai compared with other varieties. In addition, the Hibiscus flowers and leaves are naturally large, making this a daunting task for someone wishing to keep their resulting bonsai size small. However, the rewards of successfully growing a Hibiscus bonsai can be readily seen in its large flowers, which range from red, orange, yellow, white, and even purple.

Himalayan Cedar

The Himalayan Cedar is an evergreen tree that produces green needles with golden undertones. The highly prized trademark scent of the Himalayan Cedar is produced in the tree's bark and makes this one of the more popular bonsai species. A fast-growing tree, the Himalayan Cedar will grow as much as six inches per year, giving plenty of opportunity for pruning and shaping.

Hinoki Cypress

A native Japanese tree, the Hinoki Cypress features fan-shaped leaves that require regular pruning and plenty of direct sunlight. The Hinoki Cypress has delicate watering needs, requiring the perfect balance between regular watering—but without overwatering.

Honeysuckle

The Honeysuckle features bark that strips away easily, leaving interesting trunk and branch patterns that make for an attractive bonsai tree. With naturally small leaves, the Honeysuckle is an excellent choice for bonsai enthusiasts looking to create a small bonsai specimen.

Hornbeam

The Hornbeam loves indirect sunlight but cannot tolerate direct sunlight, making it an ideal bonsai to be grown indoors near a window. Your Hornbeam needs protection from frost and extreme cold temperatures.

Indian Banyan

The national tree of India, the Indian Banyan is one of the largest species of tree in the world. Due to its Indian origins, the Indian Banyan requires constant humidity and shade for much of the day but thrives best when given a shady reprieve from the sun in the afternoon. With its naturally old appearance, the Indian Banyan makes a stunning bonsai specimen.

Indian Laurel Fig

The Indian Laurel Fig is a tropical plant suited to either indoors or outdoors and prefers indirect yet bright light. With its interesting trunk shape and its willingness to be twisted and sculpted, the Indian Laurel Fig lends itself nicely to many different bonsai styles and is an excellent choice for beginners.

Jacaranda

Native to central South America, the Jacaranda features blue flowers and attractive compound leaves. Ideally suited for indoor living, the Jacaranda requires constant clean airflow and thrives when placed in a well-ventilated indoor area near a window. For best results, trim your Jacaranda regularly.

Jade

Jade is an easy-to-care-for succulent evergreen plant with thick leaves and stems and a naturally thick trunk, giving it a mature look even in its younger years. Despite a preference for sunlight, Jade can be grown either indoors or outdoors. Jade is native to Cape Town in South Africa, making it naturally drought resistant and giving it a preference for coarse, sandy soil. A low-maintenance bonsai with a naturally aged appearance, Jade is an excellent choice for beginners and can be made into an attractive bonsai in a relatively short time compared with other species.

Japanese Black Pine

Native to the coastal regions of Japan's south, the Japanese Black Pine has bark with a rough appearance and naturally long needles that grow in pairs. Reducing the length of the needles takes specialized pruning techniques, making the Japanese Black Pine best left to more experienced bonsai growers. The Japanese Black Pine has high requirements for warmth and sunlight and must be protected from frost. Relatively drought resistant, the Japanese Black Pine can survive without water for several weeks.

Japanese Flowering Cherry

With its dark, rough trunk and beautiful pink flowers, the Japanese Flowering Cherry makes a stunning deciduous bonsai. However, this Japanese native tree is prone to developing fungal diseases and is resistant to heavy root pruning. The Japanese Flowering Cherry is otherwise relatively easy to shape and prune thanks to its pliable trunk and branches.

Japanese Holly

The Japanese Holly is an evergreen shrub that bears cute white flowers and black fruit. Native to eastern Asia, the Japanese Holly is highly tolerant to pruning, making it an excellent choice for a hands-on bonsai gardener.

Japanese Maple

The Japanese Maple is a hardy deciduous tree that can be formed into several bonsai styles. Preferring to grow in a sunny location with plenty of fresh air, the Japanese Maple nevertheless requires daily shade to prevent damage to its leaves. A relatively frost-hardy tree, the Japanese Maple requires frost protection only when temperatures dip lower than -14 degrees Fahrenheit (-25 degrees Celsius). The leaves of the Japanese Maple have five pointed lobes in a distinctive hand shape. Its leaf size can be kept small with leaf pruning every second year.

Japanese White Pine (Five Needle Pine)

Native to the mountainous regions of Japan, the Japanese White Pine is a unique species of pine with blue-tinged needles that grow in bundles of five—unlike similar species with needles growing in pairs. With smooth bark and an unusual appearance, the Japanese White Pine requires frost protection and thrives in well-draining soil.

Japanese Winterberry

The Japanese Winterberry is a small deciduous shrub with pretty, light pink flowers offset by dark green leaves. When properly cared for, the flowers will give way to long-lasting red berries.

Juniper

Juniper is a genus with over 50 coniferous evergreen trees, and together these are some of the most well-known and popular types of bonsai. While the Juniper cannot tolerate indoor living conditions, it makes for an easy to care for outdoor bonsai. Choose a sunny position with afternoon shade and consider how you will protect your Juniper bonsai should temperatures dip below 14 degrees Fahrenheit (-10 degrees Celsius). The Juniper is capable of turning into a variety of bonsai styles and can make an excellent candidate for deadwood styling. Junipers are hardy trees with flexible branches and can tolerate even aggressive levels of pruning, making them a popular choice for beginners looking to build their experience in bonsai styling, shaping, wiring, and pruning.

Liquidambar

Liquidambar is an easy-to-maintain deciduous tree with a captivating branch and trunk structure, making it an ideal species for the art of bonsai. The leaves of the Liquidambar change color from season to season, ranging from bright reds and oranges to deep burgundy.

Magnolia

Magnolias make for stunning bonsai projects; however, they require a considerable level of effort to keep them at their best. The large leaves of the Magnolia can prove difficult to pare down, while the correspondingly large flowers in shades of purple, red, pink, and white are a sight to behold. Resist overwatering your Magnolia and ensure that it receives full sun exposure, as often as possible. Magnolias need to be protected from frost.

Mimosa

The Mimosa tree is an excellent choice for bonsai beginners, with its delicate appearance and fast-growing properties. Featuring fronds covered in masses of tiny leaves, the Mimosa will produce fuzzy, delicate pom-pom style flowers. Training and styling a Mimosa bonsai is an enjoyable process, as the branches and trunks grow and thicken at a relatively fast rate compared with other popular bonsai species.

Money Tree

Money Trees are a firm bonsai favorite for those who practice feng shui or who subscribe to the long-held cultural belief that Money Trees bring luck and prosperity. A highly adaptable tree with a braided trunk, Money Trees can be grown indoors or outdoors provided they can receive plenty of sunlight in a warm environment.

Mountain Pine

With its bent and often twisted trunk and durable deadwood, the Mountain Pine makes a stunning bonsai specimen. Easy to maintain and frost-resistant, the Mountain Pine is a fantastic choice for bonsai beginners but must not be overwatered.

Needle Juniper

The Needle Juniper is highly popular with beginner and more experienced bonsai growers alike due to its propensity to resemble an ancient tree even in its younger years. Easy to grow and simple to shape, the Needle Juniper is resilient when it comes to pruning and training and is easy to shape into various bonsai styles.

Norfolk Island Pine

When most people think of a Norfolk Island Pine in its natural state, they picture a giant Christmas tree—with some growing as tall as 200 feet. In its bonsai form, the Norfolk Island Pine is attractive and hardy but requires sunlight from all angles. If grown indoors, ensure that you move it from window to window—or at least rotate it regularly—to ensure an even distribution of sunlight.

Oak (Quercus)

Oak is a genus containing more than 600 different species, many of which can successfully be trained in the art of bonsai. Oak trees produce acorn nuts and tend to be strong trees that naturally grow strong and old in the wild. An Oak bonsai will need protection from Winter frost but will otherwise be capable of surviving in a wide range of climatic conditions. Root pruning an Oak tree requires a specialized set of skills and is best left to a more experienced bonsai grower to tackle.

Olive

Olive trees boast a naturally smooth trunk and have a strong branch structure, making them ideal for creating attractive bonsai. While it is possible to succeed in growing an Olive tree indoors, they perform best when outdoors in full sunlight. An Olive bonsai can tolerate short periods of drought but will struggle in frosty conditions.

Pine

Pine trees tend to grow rough, rugged appearing bark that gives them an aged appearance, making them an excellent species for the art of bonsai. A Pine bonsai will thrive in an outdoor area with plenty of fresh air and full sunlight. A resilient and highly trainable bonsai species, the Pine tree is capable of being pruned into almost any bonsai style.

Pomegranate

With its shallow root system, the Pomegranate is a fruit tree that is well-suited to the art of bonsai. Preferring to live outdoors in full sun, the Pomegranate should only be brought indoors when temperatures dip below 41 degrees Fahrenheit (5 degrees Celsius). Suitable for any bonsai style, the Pomegranate features red fruit-bearing flowers and knotted thick bark. As a bonsai, pomegranates require regular watering.

Powder Puff

Powder Puff trees feature a thick trunk offset by jade-colored leaves and delicate flowers that give the Powder Puff tree its name. Truly a stunning and resilient tree in bonsai form.

Premna

As a sub-tropical plant, the Premna requires plenty of sunlight. It is possible to grow a Premna indoors but ensure that they have a prime window position.

Privet

Privet is a genus of trees with many different species, most of which are evergreen and some of which produce variegated leaves. A genus of easy-to-maintain and robust trees, the Privet requires plenty of direct sunlight and regular trimming. Privets are fast growers and highly adaptive to different climates and bonsai pruning/wiring techniques. A well-cared-for Privet will produce pink and white flowers and black fruit.

Pyracantha

Native to Asia, the Pyracantha is a genus of shrub rather than a tree. All seven species within the genus are thorny and broadleaf and can reach heights as tall as 18 feet when grown in the wild. In bonsai form, a well-treated Pyracantha will produce delicate white flowers, which will later give way to tiny orange or red berries. An excellent choice for those wishing to grow bonsai indoors, the Pyracantha requires frequent watering.

Redwood

The Redwood is a genus of trees that includes some of the tallest tree species, effortlessly reaching heights of up to 300 feet. Native to coastal areas of Oregon and California, the Redwood loves plenty of sunlight most of the day but requires a degree of shade protection during sunny afternoons. A hardy, evergreen tree, Redwoods are popular with beginner and experienced bonsai growers alike.

Rosemary

The benefits of successfully growing a Rosemary shrub are plentiful, but they can be notoriously difficult to keep alive. Rosemary bonsais are very particular when it comes to their exposure to air, water, and sunlight, yet they make up for these difficulties by being fast, sturdy growers. Pruned areas of the Rosemary shrub can be used to garnish or season foods, or used in aromatherapy.

Sawara Cypress

A native to Japan, the Sawara Cypress is a slow-growing conifer that requires constant moisture and protection from frost.

Scots Pine

A pine species native to Europe, the Scots Pine boasts attractive red bark on its trunk and relatively thin needles compared to similar species. With delicate foliage and frost-resistant roots, the Scots Pine is relatively easy to care for. Ensure that your soil doesn't become too wet and place it in a position to receive plenty of sunlight.

Sea Grape

The Sea Grape is an evergreen flowering tree that produces ivory-colored flowers with a delicate appearance. The Sea Grape is most commonly known for the red vein that cuts through the round leaves and which eventually causes the leaf to turn completely red as the tree ages. It is this uniqueness that leads many bonsai growers to tackle the Sea Grape as a bonsai project.

Serissa

The Serissa is a temperamental tree that demands specific conditions to thrive but will reward a patient and attentive grower with year-round white flowers and glossy green leaves. When the right mixture of air, sunlight, and water is attained, the Serissa will grow vigorously and produce spiny branches that can be styled into a dome-shaped canopy.

Snow Rose

The Snow Rose shrub is native to southeast Asia and produces small, variegated leaves, tiny white flowers, and has a light-colored trunk. The Snow Rose makes a temperamental bonsai and does not do well under changing conditions. Ensure you protect your Snow Rose from frost and keep it in a warm, humid, well-lit environment at all times.

Spruce

As a coniferous evergreen tree, the Spruce requires protection from frost and freezing temperatures, as well as plenty of sunlight. Apart from these specific growing conditions, the Spruce is an easy-to-maintain bonsai tree.

Trident Maple

The Trident Maple is native to Eastern China, Taiwan, and Japan. It is considered a particularly robust and beginner-friendly bonsai species. As a strictly outdoors tree, the Trident Maple requires protection from direct sunlight and frost but can otherwise endure a range of tough conditions, including air pollution and dry soil. As a fast-growing tree, it needs regular trimming. This is one of my favorite bonsai tree options.

Water Jasmine

Native to Malaysia and China, the Water Jasmine can grow up to 20 feet tall in the wild. With prominent and noticeable surface roots and smooth light-colored bark, the Water Jasmine makes for an attractive specimen when trained as a bonsai.

Weeping Fig

The Weeping Fig is a popular choice for bonsai beginners and experienced growers alike, especially those looking to experiment with various pruning techniques. This versatile evergreen tree grows glossy leaves that are naturally small and can easily be pruned into an umbrella-style canopy. With a preference for at least six hours of sunlight per day and ongoing moist soil, the Weeping Fig features twisted surface roots that make for an attractive bonsai project.

Weeping Willow

A native of China, the Weeping Willow can be found throughout the northern hemisphere. Its long, yellow drooping branches can reach as far down as the ground and give the tree its name. Weeping Willows are generally best reserved for more experienced bonsai artists due to their difficulty in styling. It is rare for a Weeping Willow to live longer than 25 years.

Wisteria

While the Wisteria is a shrub rather than a tree, it creates a stunning bonsai with purple, blue, white, or violet flowers. Wisterias prefer full, direct sunlight and can be grown in various parts of the world. While a relatively easy tree to maintain, Wisterias will not begin to produce their trademark flowers until they are around ten years old—a feature that turns many people away from this unique bonsai choice.

Zelkova

Native to Japan and China, the Zelkova genus includes two species that can successfully be turned into bonsai projects. A favorite with beginners, Zelkova bonsai trees are less likely to succumb to common bonsai diseases and pests and are renowned for being sturdy, resilient trees. Most commonly associated with the broom bonsai style, Zelkova trees are deciduous and change their leaf colors seasonally.

13

Chapter 13: Presentation & Display

How and Where to Present Your Bonsai

Growing bonsai trees can seem like a lonely pursuit—until you enter the world of bonsai clubs, exhibitions, and competitions. I highly recommend that all bonsai growers—regardless of their age, demographic, or location—find and join a bonsai group. Bonsai Empire has put together a fantastic resource to help people find bonsai groups all around the world: www.bonsaiempire.com/locations/clubs

Many people enjoy being part of a real-life bonsai club as well as becoming active in online bonsai websites, social media groups, chat rooms, and forums.

Not only will joining a bonsai club put you in contact with fellow bonsai enthusiasts in your local area or online, but it will give you access to an abundance of resources. The best way to improve your bonsai skills is through time, practice, and learning from people more experienced than you. At a bonsai club, you will have the opportunity to showcase your handiwork, ask questions, gain valuable knowledge, and later pass on some of your learnings to new members.

Most bonsai groups also organize or partake in competitions and exhibitions, giving you further valuable opportunities to showcase your bonsai trees and receive feedback from more experienced growers.

Stands and Accessories

Bonsai trees are a work of art, and as such, are designed to be seen! Displaying your bonsai is a crucial element of its overall creation. When considering how best to display your bonsai, keep in mind that, while there are companion items and unique displays that can complement your arrangement, your bonsai must always be the focal point of your arrangement. Remember too that your display should invoke a sense of harmony and nature, and that every element of your bonsai display must be well thought out and intentional.

Choosing a Bonsai Stand, Shelf, or Table

Bonsai trees are best appreciated at eye level. Keep this critical element in mind when choosing a stand, shelf, or table to display your bonsai. The display furniture you choose should be sufficiently natural and understated in its design, in that it does not seek to distract from the bonsai tree itself. Choose your furniture's material and color carefully to ensure that it remains in harmony with the natural elements of your bonsai. Natural dark woods tend to suit many bonsai, while lighter woods can be the perfect choice for flowering bonsai.

Companion Objects

While not strictly necessary, many bonsai displays include carefully chosen companion objects, such as stones intended to represent mountains (suiseki), a hanging scroll (kakemono), a small statue, or a smaller complimentary plant. At most, two companion objects can be chosen. Any more and your display can seem cluttered.

Arranging your Display

If your bonsai is symmetrical, it should likely be placed in the middle of the display. However, if your bonsai tree leans predominantly to one side, place the tree on the opposite side of the display to balance its appearance. A companion objection should not be located too close to the bonsai and must not be on the same horizontal line. If you use stones in your display, these should be placed towards the back of the display to represent distant mountains.

Chapter 14: FAQs

Bonsai Basics

Can any tree be turned into a bonsai?

Almost any type of tree—as well as several types of shrubs, plants, and vines—can be turned into a bonsai. A bonsai is not a particular tree species like an Apple tree or an Oak tree. The word instead refers to the methods used to train the tree to live in a small container and to resemble a miniature version of its full-size counterpart and in a certain desired style.

How tall should a bonsai tree be?

There are no restrictions on how tall or short a bonsai should be. Bonsai competitions usually feature different size and category classes in which bonsai growers can compete, but a tree of any height can be considered a bonsai if it is grown in a container and conforms to other bonsai standards.

How long can a bonsai tree live?

Bonsai trees can easily live just as long as the same tree species in the wild. There have been many instances where a bonsai has exceeded its natural lifespan simply due to the high levels of specialized care offered to the tree. Some bonsai trees are estimated to be more than 800 years old, which have been passed down through multiple generations of families.

What is the most expensive bonsai tree?

To date, the most expensive bonsai tree on record was a white pine tree that was many centuries old and was sold for over US $1.3 million at the International Bonsai Convention in Takamatsu, Japan. Of course, other bonsai trees are so highly valued that their owners refuse to sell them, effectively making their worth unknown.

How are bonsai trees kept so small?

Specialized horticultural techniques are employed to train bonsai trees into their miniatured form and to keep them small while they continue to mature. These techniques include growing the bonsai tree in a shallow container; pruning, trimming, and grafting the branches, roots, trunk, and leaves as needed; and repotting the tree regularly.

How can I find out the age of a bonsai tree?

The simplest way of estimating the age of a bonsai is to measure the diameter of its trunk and compare that to the overall growth of the tree. A more accurate idea of the bonsai tree's age can be estimated by taking a core sample of the tree's trunk or by counting its growth rings, but don't cut your tree down for this purpose!

How much is my bonsai tree worth?

Bonsai trees can range in value from inexpensive to hundreds of thousands of dollars. While there is no one way of determining the value of a bonsai, factors to consider include the bonsai tree's age and species, the design and quality of its trunk, branches, leaves, and roots, and its overall artistic appeal. Ultimately, a bonsai is only worth what someone is willing to pay for it. Much will depend on the artistic merit of the bonsai.

Why doesn't my tree look like a bonsai?

While there is certainly a stereotypical bonsai style that many people associate with the art of bonsai, keep in mind that any tree grown in a shallow container that conforms to bonsai standards is a true bonsai —even if the species itself is an unusual one like a plant, shrub, or even a vine.

Getting Started

How can I get started growing bonsai trees?

There are several ways to start nurturing a bonsai. You could purchase an existing bonsai tree from a reputable nursery or experienced grower and take over the care of an existing tree. You could purchase a small sapling—known as a pre-bonsai—and begin the growing process, or you could even start by germinating your bonsai from a seed. Keep in mind that it will take several years before a pre-bonsai and one grown from a seed will be large enough to begin wiring, shaping, and styling. If you are keen to start developing these skills straight away, it may be a good idea to purchase an already established bonsai tree.

What is the single most important piece of advice for a bonsai beginner?

Perfecting the practice of bonsai is all about patience and persistence. No one is born with the skills to create bonsai works of art, and no one can shortcut the learning process. Know that you will inevitably make mistakes that will damage or even kill one or more of your bonsai trees. Promise yourself that you will be persistent and learn from your mistakes rather than give up after the first setback. Every setback is a setup for a comeback.

What is the best bonsai for a beginner to start with?

Beginner bonsai growers should first look toward species that naturally grow in similar climatic conditions to where they live. For example, while the Adenium tree is well-regarded as an excellent bonsai for beginners, it is native to Africa and Arabia. Unless you live in an area with a similar climate to this tree's native home, your tree may struggle to thrive. Similarly, decide in advance whether you plan to keep your bonsai indoors or outdoors, as this will dramatically affect your choice. Tree species that may be suitable for beginners include the Boxwood, Buttonwood, Ficus, Hawaiian Umbrella, Jade, Juniper, Mimosa, and Redwood, amongst others mentioned in the previous chapter.

Is it expensive to buy a ready-made bonsai tree?

The price of a bonsai tree is determined by its age and quality, as well as its sentimental value. When purchasing a high-quality bonsai, you are in effect remunerating the seller for the years of care, pruning, watering, and fertilizing that has gone into creating the product you're buying. To avoid paying exorbitant prices for an established bonsai, consider growing your own bonsai from a sapling (known as a pre-bonsai) but be aware that it can take several years before your bonsai has grown large enough to begin shaping and pruning.

Should I buy a ready-made bonsai tree with rocks glued on it?

While it is legitimate to purchase an established bonsai tree and take over its care, it is always a good idea to avoid purchasing ready-made bonsai trees that have rocks glued to their soil. The sight of the glued rocks should be a clear warning sign that this bonsai has been mass-produced and has not been given the individual care and attention that every healthy bonsai needs.

Mass-produced bonsai trees are typically made by taking cuttings from a host plant and rooting the cuttings in an Asian-style pot. Trees constructed in such a way tend to be both vulnerable and fragile. Rocks glued to the soil prevent water evaporation and soil disturbances during transit, ensuring that those selling these mass-produced trees do not have to take the time to regularly water and otherwise tend to them. Keeping in mind that bonsai trees do not perform well with soggy or muddy soil, it stands to reason that mass-produced bonsai trees with water trapped by a layer of rocks and glue will be unhealthy and susceptible to root rot and fungus growth. Most bonsais created and sold in this way simply will not survive long term.

How long does it take to grow a bonsai?

If you are growing a bonsai from a seed or a sapling (also known as a pre-bonsai), it can take several years before your tree is large and established enough to begin trimming, pruning, and shaping it. The beauty of a bonsai comes down to its artistic style and the amount of time and care that has been invested in its growth. With experience and care, it is possible to grow a beautiful bonsai tree in three or four years.

How hard is it to grow and take care of a bonsai?

There is a common misconception that growing and maintaining a bonsai tree is difficult. In reality, it is no more challenging to keep a bonsai alive than any other tree/houseplant—provided you have chosen a tree species that can survive in your particular climate and have placed it in an optimal position. The difficulty of bonsai typically comes down to the artistic aspect of the practice, which involves setting a vision for the aesthetics of your tree and patiently pruning, trimming, and shaping to achieve your vision.

Do I need to be an experienced gardener to grow bonsai trees?

While having pre-existing gardening skills may flatten the learning curve a little, it is not a requirement to be an experienced gardener before taking up the art of bonsai. The more you practice and experiment with growing bonsai trees, the faster your skills and expertise will accumulate.

Is the art of bonsai accessible?

Bonsai is a very accessible art, especially compared to other forms of horticulture. Little physical work is required to establish and care for a bonsai tree, making this practice accessible to people who may otherwise be put off by heavy lifting or using power tools. Bonsai is widely held to be a form of meditative relaxation, making it a wonderful practice for easing anxiety and other mental health issues. Similarly, children can gain great enjoyment from nurturing a bonsai and may need only a little assistance or supervision to ensure the tree is cared for correctly.

Do I need a garden to grow a bonsai tree?

You don't need a garden to grow a bonsai. If growing an outdoor bonsai, you only need a small outdoor area that receives plenty of sunlight to position your pot. Otherwise, choose one of the tree species that can tolerate living indoors.

The Perfect Home

Should my bonsai tree live indoors or outdoors?

Several tree species can survive perfectly well indoors. However, if possible, all indoor bonsai trees should have the opportunity to spend some time outdoors—especially during the Summer. Your number one priority when growing a bonsai should always be the strength and vitality of your tree. As natural specimens that would normally grow outdoors in the wild, all trees can benefit from time spent outdoors.

Is it easier to keep a bonsai tree indoors or outdoors?

While it may seem easier to keep a tree indoors than outdoors, the opposite is usually true. Indoor plants are forced to survive and thrive in an artificial environment and must be more constantly observed to ensure they are receiving ample rays of sunlight, airflow, and humidity.

How much sunlight does my bonsai need?

The sunlight requirements of your bonsai will depend on its specific species. Make sure you are familiar with the specific requirements of your bonsai and follow the earlier recommendations for your tree, or check online for more information. As a guide, however, remember that trees naturally grow outdoors in the wild, where they receive sunlight and proper air circulation. If you are unsure about your bonsai tree's sunlight requirements, find out where your particular tree species would grow in the wild and do your best to emulate those conditions for your bonsai.

What are the ideal conditions for an indoor bonsai?

The exact conditions required by your bonsai tree will vary according to its species, but in general, indoor bonsai trees benefit from being kept on a windowsill where they can receive as much sunlight as possible—but away from artificial heat sources like a central heating vent or indoor fireplace. Ideally, keep your bonsai tree within one foot of the window. Any further away and the power of the sun's rays will decrease dramatically. If you don't have windows that provide sufficient sunlight, you might want to consider using a grow light to sustain your tree indoors.

How do I provide my bonsai with sufficient humidity?

If you feel that your bonsai isn't receiving the level of humidity it would otherwise receive in the wild, consider using a humidity tray. Add some rocks to the bottom of the humidity tray to ensure that your bonsai sits above the water and not in it. This helps to prevent your roots from becoming waterlogged. As the water in the humidity tray evaporates, a humid environment will be created. Forget about misting your bonsai to create humidity, as the effects will last for only a short time.

How can I protect my bonsai from frost and extreme cold?

The ideal location for a bonsai tree during the coldest months of the year is an unheated greenhouse. However, since most people don't have easy access to a greenhouse, there are other methods you can use to provide adequate protection. The aim is to insulate the bonsai tree's roots from the cold, and you can achieve this in several ways. Consider wrapping the bonsai tree pot in bubble wrap with the bubbles on the pot side and taping it in place. Alternatively, try burying the pot underground (with the tree above ground).

What should I do with my bonsai when I go on vacation?

This answer depends on the species of your bonsai and how long you will be away. Some tree species will tolerate short periods of drought or neglect, while many species need constant care. If you are away for more than a couple of days, it will likely be necessary to find someone to take care of your bonsai while you're away. Ensure that you leave specific instructions for your bonsai tree's care while you're gone and choose someone who will follow your instructions without hesitation.

Fertilizing and Watering

What do I feed my bonsai?

Bonsai trees are fed using a special fertilizer mixture that has been specifically formulated to provide bonsai trees with the nutrients they need to thrive. Refer to Chapter 7 for detailed information on fertilization.

How often (when) should I feed my bonsai?

Only feed your bonsai tree during its growing season and never during Winter dormancy. When bonsai trees are fertilized during their Winter dormancy, the fertilizer will either be wasted or will prompt the tree to come out of dormancy too early. The frequency of feeding will depend on your individual tree's species, but as a general guide, you'll need to fertilize your bonsai once a week during Spring and Summer, then reduce the frequency to monthly during the Fall. Older trees generally do not need to be fertilized as often as younger trees, as their rate of growth will have significantly slowed.

Are there any times when I should not feed my bonsai?

If you feel that your bonsai is not in good health or is dying, temporarily stop fertilizing your tree until it has returned to health. Similarly, stop fertilizing your bonsai if it is under stress for reasons such as recent pruning or wiring. If your bonsai tree is in Winter dormancy, it is a good idea to stop fertilizing since fertilizer encourages growth which may bring it out of dormancy, when the plant should be resting. Finally, hold off fertilizing your bonsai for several weeks after it has been repotted to give it a chance to settle in and adapt to its new environment.

How often should I water my bonsai?

Your bonsai tree's watering schedule will vary depending on its species, its present health, and whether it is being kept indoors or outdoors, making it key to understand your particular tree and its ideal growing conditions. However, even if you find the suggested watering schedule for your individual tree species, never water your tree based on a fixed schedule. Instead, get to know the normal condition of your bonsai soil and start a habit of checking the condition of the soil with your index finger.

With experience, you will also be able to test the condition of the soil by feeling the weight of the pot, as the pot will feel lighter when the soil is dry. When you notice the soil drying out, water your bonsai and ensure that the root mass is thoroughly wet. Don't water your bonsai again until the soil shows signs of becoming dry.

How do I know if I'm watering too much or too little?

Watering too much or too little can cause your bonsai tree to die. If your bonsai is suffering from a lack of water, the effects will be seen relatively quickly. The roots will begin to collapse, leading to the foliage looking dry. Avoid underwatering by paying attention to the state of the bonsai tree's soil. In the case of overwatering, the effects may take a little longer to notice. The roots will become waterlogged and the health of your entire bonsai will begin to decline. Avoid overwatering by ensuring that your bonsai tree's drainage system is working well and that the root ball is not too thick. Otherwise, it will begin retaining water.

Pruning and Shaping

When should I start trimming and pruning my bonsai?

The objective of trimming and pruning is to ensure that your bonsai stays small and achieves its desired shape. As such, shaping should begin when the tree is young and still maturing. Doing this will ensure that all of your future shapings are more about maintaining the initial shape, rather than allowing the tree to grow uncontrollably at first and having to make major shaping changes in the future.

How often do I need to prune my bonsai?

Regular pruning will help keep your bonsai tree's development under control and allow you to set its shape and style while the tree is still young. Deciduous trees tend to be hardy species and usually need to be trimmed more often than evergreen trees.

How often should I cut my bonsai tree's roots?

This will depend on your tree species, but, as a general guide, every two or three years the roots of your bonsai will fill the pot. When this occurs, the roots will need to be trimmed and reduced, and fresh bonsai soil should be added.

How do I shape a bonsai tree?

Bonsai trees are shaped using the techniques of trimming, pruning, and wiring. Pruning will usually be done several times a year, depending on the age and the species of your tree. It takes time and patience to learn how to shape a bonsai tree, and the only way to develop these skills is to practice and be persistent.

How do I train my bonsai?

Bonsai trees are trained using wiring, a technique that involves moving the trunk or branches of your bonsai into the desired position and using wire to hold the trunk or branch in place. The wire is later removed after the branches have had a chance to hold themselves in their new position.

Do I need to buy expensive tools to shape my bonsai?

When you're first getting started with the art of bonsai, it can seem daunting to comprehend the vast number of tools and other equipment that experienced bonsai growers use—especially when you consider that these experienced bonsai growers prefer expensive imported tools from Japan. However, there is no need to purchase a multitude of expensive items when you're first getting started. It is possible to buy inexpensive or second-hand tools that will perform just as well as new tools. Additionally, you'll find that you won't need a full set of tools right away and can gradually add to your collection over time. If you decide to continue with the art of bonsai in years to come, you can, of course, replace your worn-out inexpensive tools with more professional, high-quality tools.

Why can't I use regular craft scissors to prune my bonsai?

It is certainly plausible to prune a bonsai with craft scissors, however, I don't recommend it. Bonsai tools are constructed with a small-angled blade, allowing you to slice through the branch without causing damage to the remaining stub. Craft scissors, on the other hand, have blades with a large angle that puts pressure on the remaining stub, causing it to compress and become damaged. This damage can lead to permanent scarring or even die-back.

Can I prune and shape during Summer?

While it will depend on the climate and the tree in question, most bonsai growers avoid pruning, wiring, shaping, and repotting during the Summer, especially during a heat wave, when trees often are in a state of dormancy and vulnerable to change.

Soil and Repotting

Why are bonsai trees grown in shallow pots?

Bonsais are usually grown in shallow pots to allow for excess water to drain away, preventing roots from becoming waterlogged. Shallow pots also add to the aesthetic appeal of a beautiful bonsai tree. For a tree that is used to living in a larger container, it can take several repottings over many years to acclimatize the bonsai to life in a smaller pot.

Can I plant my bonsai in regular potting or garden soil?

Unlike house plants, bonsai trees do not perform well in soil that stays soggy, muddy, or overly wet. Consistently wet soil can cause root rot, which is one of the most common reasons for bonsai trees to die. For this reason, it is best to avoid typical potting mix or gardening soil that would otherwise suit indoor potted plants. Instead, specially formulated bonsai soil allows for water to freely drain away from the tree and its roots while retaining just the right degree of moisture and essential aeration to promote a healthy bonsai. A good tip is to cover your bonsai pot's drainage holes with mesh or screening to allow water to pass through while preventing any soil from leaking out.

Do different trees require different types of soil?

While all bonsai trees require soil that drains freely while retaining moisture, the individual bonsai soil mixture will vary between tree species.

When is the best time to repot my bonsai tree?

In general, the best time to repot a bonsai tree is in early Spring when the tree is still in its Winter dormancy. Repotting can cause stress to a bonsai, and this stress will be minimized if the task is completed when the tree is not in its growing phase and is not yet sustaining its full Summer foliage.

How often does my bonsai need to be repotted?

Several factors will dictate how often your bonsai needs to be repotted, including the species of your tree, the local climate, the age of your bonsai, and the size of its current pot. Luckily, there is a simple way of checking whether your bonsai is ready to be repotted. Carefully lift your bonsai out of its pot and observe the roots. If the roots are forming a circle at the bottom of the pot, it is time to repot.

When should I completely replace my bonsai tree's soil?

It is a good idea to completely replace your bonsai tree's soil when you repot your bonsai. As a general guide, this should happen every two to three years.

Troubleshooting and Diseases

How can I tell if my bonsai is still alive?

If your bonsai tree has been struggling to thrive for some time or has been infested with a pest or disease, it can be difficult to tell if it is still alive. A simple way to know if your bonsai is still alive is to perform a scratch test of the bark of your bonsai. Using a fingernail, scratch away a tiny portion of bark. If the underlying layer is green, your bonsai is still alive. If you see a dried-out layer underneath the bark, your bonsai may be beyond the point of saving.

Why does my bonsai look unhealthy in Winter?

While it's always a good idea to stay vigilant and be on the lookout for any pests or diseases that could be plaguing your bonsai tree, it's also worth remembering that some bonsai trees may appear to be in poor health during the Winter. In a similar way to trees growing in nature, some bonsai trees will appear sparse and even shorter during the coldest months of the year because of the inevitable lack of sunlight during Winter months. When this occurs, your bonsai tree should return to its former strength and beauty in Spring and continue to grow and flourish during Summer.

What are the main causes of a dead or dying bonsai?

Water and sunlight—either too much or too little—are the usual suspects when a bonsai tree is dying. While other mistakes like aggressive pruning or incorrect repotting practices can cause a bonsai to die, in most instances, bonsai trees die from issues relating to water or sunlight.

The leaves of my bonsai are falling off. Is my bonsai dying?

When your bonsai starts losing leaves, first ask yourself: Is my bonsai tree species a deciduous one? If the answer is yes, it is natural for the leaves of your bonsai to change color and fall off during the Fall. However, if your tree is not deciduous or the leaf shedding is occurring during Summer or Spring, losing leaves could signal that your tree is under stress. Also, check to ensure that your tree is placed in a position to benefit from optimal sunlight and that it is receiving adequate water, fertilizer, and free air.

Why has my bonsai developed spots on its leaves?

When your bonsai develops spots or other unusual marks on its leaves, your tree may be infected with a disease or fungal infection. Act fast to remove the diseased leaves and treat the remainder of your tree. It is best to get professional advice when you suspect your tree is diseased to increase the likelihood that your tree can be saved.

How can I prevent insects and diseases from damaging my bonsai?

The best way to prevent insects and diseases from harming your bonsai is to keep your tree healthy and strong as a weak or unhealthy tree is more likely to be attacked by insects or infected with a disease.

Other preventative measures include ensuring that your bonsai receives plenty of sunlight and fresh air, keeping the soil clear of fallen leaves and flowers, and ensuring that the soil does not become muddy or waterlogged. However, despite your best efforts, diseases and insects can potentially infest any bonsai tree. It is important that you stay vigilant and be on the lookout for anything that could be making your tree unhealthy.

15

Conclusion

You've almost reached the end of the book, congratulations! Now is an opportune time to think back to the knowledge (or lack thereof) you had about growing bonsai trees when you first started reading this book. Perhaps you were feeling nervous and worried that you would never be able to learn everything you need to know to successfully grow a bonsai tree without killing it.

Now that you've reached this point, you can see how much you have learned along the way. Your eyes have been opened to the beautiful world of bonsai trees, and you now understand that—while bonsai trees do require constant love and care—practicing this art isn't as difficult as you may have been led to believe.

In this book, we covered every important aspect of growing bonsai trees. We started with the benefits of bonsai growing and the deep, rich history behind the practice. We looked at the various types of bonsai tree species—both in generalities and by considering some of the most popular and rewarding species in particular. Next came a detailed list of all the tools and equipment you would need to grow bonsai trees, along with an indication of price points for various items.

Then came the practical skills section. We covered every element you need to keep your bonsai tree alive, from planting and choosing bonsai soil, to fertilizing and watering. We looked at styling, shaping, and pruning, including repotting and creating artistic deadwood. Finally, we covered the troubleshooting section, seeking always to cover every question or concern you could conceivably have during your time as a bonsai grower.

The onus now shifts to you. Will you take this knowledge and apply it to one or more bonsai trees of your own? Getting started with bonsai trees doesn't have to be difficult or expensive. As Chapter 4 explained, there are plenty of ways to source your first bonsai tree without breaking the bank. You have the information—it is simply time for you to start experiencing the world of bonsai trees firsthand.

I also hope by reading this book and practicing the skills and lessons, you will gain the patience, determination, and persistence needed to truly succeed long-term in the art of bonsai. It's a great feeling to know that you can grow trees that will re-energize your home and improve your mental well-being. Hopefully, you will also gain the skills and experience to nurture your own bonsai tree to create a lifelong companion and living heirloom that can start with you and be passed down for generations to come.

It is my hope and dearest wish that more people will come to love and understand bonsai trees the way that I do. That is why I wrote this book.

I wish you the best of luck on your journey.

Clive Woods

16

Resources & Bibliography

3 Essential Bonsai Tools For Beginners. (2018, December 16). Retrieved January 20, 2021, from https://www.basicbonsai.com/3-essential-bonsai-tools-for-beginners/

5 Bonsai Mistakes That Are Killing Your Tree. (2019, June 20). Retrieved January 20, 2021, from https://www.basicbonsai.com/5-bonsai-mistakes/

13 Types of Bonsai Trees (by Style and Shape Plus Pictures). (2020, June 25). Retrieved January 17, 2021, from https://www.homestratosphere.com/pictures-bonsai-trees/

14 Different Types of Bonsai Tree Growing Tools. (2021, January 13). Retrieved January 16, 2021, from https://www.homestratosphere.com/types-of-bonsai-tree-growing-tools/

22 Best Trees For Bonsai | Best Bonsai Plants. (2019, December 6). Retrieved January 20, 2021, from https://balconygardenweb.com/best-trees-for-bonsai-best-bonsai-plants/

A Guide to Buying Bonsai Tools. (2017, April 29). Retrieved January 16, 2021, from https://treehighbonsai.wordpress.com/2017/04/12/a-guide-to-buying-bonsai-tools/

A Guide to Choosing a Pot For Your Bonsai Tree. (2021, January 4). Retrieved January 16, 2021, from https://www.bonsai-en.com.au/post/a-guide-to-choosing-a-pot-for-your-bonsai-tree

Adams, J. (1998, May). Basic Tools for Bonsai. Retrieved January 16, 2021, from https://www.bonsai-bci.com/tools/article.html

Akin, C. (2020a, December 30). The 6 Best Indoor Bonsai Tree Types & How To Care For Them. Retrieved January 15, 2021, from https://bonsairesourcecenter.com/the-6-best-indoor-bonsai-tree-types-how-to-care-for-them/

Akin, C. (2020b, December 30). The Best Bonsai Tree Benefits for Your Body and Soul. Retrieved January 15, 2021, from https://bonsairesourcecenter.com/the-best-bonsai-tree-benefits-for-your-body-and-soul/

Anyone had any experiences buying a bonsai online? (2011, September 5). Retrieved January 16, 2021, from https://www.reddit.com/r/Bonsai/comments/k5flj/anyone_had_any_experiences_buying_a_bonsai_online/

Avoid Winter damage in bonsai: Rain – Growing Bonsai. (2017, November 24). Retrieved January 18, 2021, from https://www.growingbonsai.net/avoid-Winter-damage-in-bonsai-rain/

Baessler, L. (n.d.). Bonsai Aquarium Plants – How To Grow Aqua Bonsai Trees. Retrieved January 16, 2021, from https://www.gardeningknowhow.com/houseplants/bonsai/bonsai-aquarium-plants.htm

Bagmoth. (n.d.). Retrieved January 18, 2021, from https://www.bonsaiforbeginners.com/bagmoth.html

Baran, R. (n.d.). All the Primary Plants Used As Bonsai and In the Related Arts. Retrieved January 20, 2021, from http://www.magiminiland.org/BigPicture/BPAIndex.html

Basic Bonsai Tree Care. (2020, April 2). Bonsai Tree care Basics | Basic Bonsai Tree Care. Retrieved January 16, 2021, from https://www.basic-bonsai-tree-care.com/bonsai-tree-care-basics/

Beaulieu, D. (2019, October 24). Defining Broadleaf Trees, Shrubs, and Other Plants. Retrieved January 15, 2021, from https://www.thespruce.com/broadleaf-plants-overview-2131014

Beaulieu, D. (2020, October 21). What Does "Deciduous" Mean? Retrieved January 15, 2021, from https://www.thespruce.com/deciduous-meaning-lists-of-examples-2131036

Benefits of Joining a Bonsai Club. (2017, November 1). Retrieved January 20, 2021, from https://blog.easternleaf.com/benefits-of-joining-a-bonsai-club/

Bonsai Empire. (2013a, July 8). How Big is Bonsai? Retrieved January 15, 2021, from https://www.bonsaiempire.com/blog/bonsai-interest-worldwide

Bonsai Empire. (2013b, August 9). Bonsai in the Karate Kid movie. Retrieved January 15, 2021, from https://www.bonsaiempire.com/blog/karate-kid-bonsai

Bonsai Empire. (2015, April 16). Help! My Bonsai is dying! Retrieved January 18, 2021, from https://www.bonsaiempire.com/blog/revive-dying-bonsai

Bonsai Empire. (2016, March 24). Aqua Bonsai. Retrieved January 16, 2021, from https://www.bonsaiempire.com/blog/aqua-bonsai

Bonsai Empire. (n.d.-a). Air layering. Retrieved January 17, 2021, from https://www.bonsaiempire.com/basics/cultivation/advanced/air-layering

Bonsai Empire. (n.d.-b). An overview of Bonsai clubs near you - Bonsai Empire. Retrieved January 20, 2021, from https://www.bonsaiempire.com/locations/clubs

Bonsai Empire. (n.d.-c). Bonsai defoliation. Retrieved January 17, 2021, from https://www.bonsaiempire.com/basics/styling/advanced/defoliation

Bonsai Empire. (n.d.-d). Bonsai FAQ. Retrieved January 20, 2021, from https://www.bonsaiempire.com/basics/general/faq

Bonsai Empire. (n.d.-e). Bonsai forest. Retrieved January 16, 2021, from https://www.bonsaiempire.com/basics/styling/advanced/forest-planting

Bonsai Empire. (n.d.-f). Bonsai pots. Retrieved January 16, 2021, from https://www.bonsaiempire.com/basics/bonsai-care/advanced/choosing-pots

Bonsai Empire. (n.d.-g). Bonsai soil. Retrieved January 16, 2021, from https://www.bonsaiempire.com/basics/bonsai-care/bonsai-soil

Bonsai Empire. (n.d.-h). Bonsai styles. Retrieved January 17, 2021, from https://www.bonsaiempire.com/origin/bonsai-styles

Bonsai Empire. (n.d.-i). Bonsai tools. Retrieved January 16, 2021, from https://www.bonsaiempire.com/basics/general/tools

Bonsai Empire. (n.d.-j). Bonsai tree care and maintenance - Bonsai Empire. Retrieved January 16, 2021, from https://www.bonsaiempire.com/basics/bonsai-care

Bonsai Empire. (n.d.-k). Buying Bonsai trees. Retrieved January 15, 2021, from https://www.bonsaiempire.com/basics/cultivation/buying-bonsai

Bonsai Empire. (n.d.-l). Buying nursery stock. Retrieved January 16, 2021, from https://www.bonsaiempire.com/basics/cultivation/nursery-stock

Bonsai Empire. (n.d.-m). Collecting trees (Yamadori). Retrieved January 16, 2021, from https://www.bonsaiempire.com/basics/cultivation/collecting-trees

Bonsai Empire. (n.d.-n). Common tree species used for Bonsai - Bonsai Empire. Retrieved January 20, 2021, from https://www.bonsaiempire.com/tree-species

Bonsai Empire. (n.d.-o). Fertilizing Bonsai. Retrieved January 16, 2021, from https://www.bonsaiempire.com/basics/bonsai-care/fertilizing

Bonsai Empire. (n.d.-p). Grafting trees. Retrieved January 16, 2021, from https://www.bonsaiempire.com/basics/cultivation/advanced/grafting-trees

Bonsai Empire. (n.d.-q). Growing a Bonsai from cuttings. Retrieved January 16, 2021, from https://www.bonsaiempire.com/basics/cultivation/from-cuttings

Bonsai Empire. (n.d.-r). History of Bonsai. Retrieved January 15, 2021, from https://www.bonsaiempire.com/origin/bonsai-history

Bonsai Empire. (n.d.-s). How to grow a Bonsai tree, for beginners - Bonsai Empire. Retrieved January 15, 2021, from https://www.bonsaiempire.com/basics

Bonsai Empire. (n.d.-t). Identify my tree. Retrieved January 15, 2021, from https://www.bonsaiempire.com/tree-species/bonsai-identification

Bonsai Empire. (n.d.-u). Identify my tree. Retrieved January 15, 2021, from https://www.bonsaiempire.com/tree-species/bonsai-identification#pines-conifers

Bonsai Empire. (n.d.-w). OverWintering your Bonsai trees. Retrieved January 18, 2021, from https://www.bonsaiempire.com/basics/bonsai-care/advanced/overWintering

Bonsai Empire. (n.d.-x). Pests and diseases. Retrieved January 18, 2021, from https://www.bonsaiempire.com/basics/bonsai-care/advanced/pests-diseases

Bonsai Empire. (n.d.-y). Placement of your trees. Retrieved January 16, 2021, from https://www.bonsaiempire.com/basics/bonsai-care/position

Bonsai Empire. (n.d.-z). Pruning Bonsai. Retrieved January 17, 2021, from https://www.bonsaiempire.com/basics/styling/pruning

Bonsai Empire. (n.d.-aa). Repotting Bonsai. Retrieved January 17, 2021, from https://www.bonsaiempire.com/basics/bonsai-care/repotting

Bonsai Empire. (n.d.-ab). Surface roots (Nebari). Retrieved January 17, 2021, from https://www.bonsaiempire.com/basics/styling/advanced/root-flare

Bonsai Empire. (n.d.-ac). Watering Bonsai trees. Retrieved January 16, 2021, from https://www.bonsaiempire.com/basics/bonsai-care/watering

Bonsai Empire. (n.d.-ad). What is Bonsai? Retrieved January 13, 2021, from https://www.bonsaiempire.com/origin/what-is-bonsai

Bonsai Empire. (n.d.-ae). Wiring Bonsai trees. Retrieved January 17, 2021, from https://www.bonsaiempire.com/basics/styling/wiring

Bonsai FAQ. (n.d.). Retrieved January 20, 2021, from https://www.bonsaiboy.com/catalog/bonsaiboyfaq.html

Bonsai for Beginners: The Definitive Guide. (2018, August 3). Retrieved January 16, 2021, from https://blog.flowersacrosssydney.com.au/bonsai-for-beginners/

Bonsai Group planting. (n.d.). Retrieved January 16, 2021, from https://www.bonsaiforbeginners.com/bonsai_groupplanting.html

Bonsai Learning Center. (2016, November 30). Selecting Containers For Bonsai | Bonsai Learning Center. Retrieved January 16, 2021, from https://bonsailearningcenter.com/2016/11/containers/

Bonsai Myths. (n.d.). Retrieved January 20, 2021, from http://www.yamadori.com/bonsai-myths/

Bonsai Outlet. (2015, July 24). The Five Best Reasons To Bring A Bonsai Tree Into Your Life. Retrieved January 15, 2021, from https://www.bonsaioutlet.com/bonsai-articles/the-five-best-reasons-to-bring-a-bonsai-tree-into-your-life/

Bonsai Outlet. (n.d.). Bonsai Soil FAQ's. Retrieved January 20, 2021, from https://www.bonsaioutlet.com/bonsai-soil-faqs/

Bonsai Pruning - How to Shape Your Bonsai. (n.d.). Retrieved January 17, 2021, from https://www.bonsai-and-blooms.com/bonsai-pruning.html

Bonsai Repotting Mistakes to Avoid Eastern Lef Knowledge Center. (2019, April 26). Retrieved January 20, 2021, from https://blog.easternleaf.com/2-bonsai-repotting-mistakes-to-avoid/

Bonsai Soil FAQs. (n.d.). Retrieved January 16, 2021, from https://www.bonsaioutlet.com/bonsai-soil-faqs/

Bonsai Tree Diseases - How to Treat Bonsai Health Issues. (n.d.). Retrieved January 18, 2021, from https://www.bonsai-and-blooms.com/bonsai-tree-diseases.html

Bonsai tree species | Bonsaischule Wenddorf. (n.d.). Retrieved January 20, 2021, from https://www.bonsai-shop.com/en/species

Bonsai Warehouse. (n.d.). Bonsai Tools. Retrieved January 16, 2021, from https://www.bonsaiwarehouse.com.au/bonsai-supplies/bonsai-tools/

Bonsaiko, T. (2017a, June 18). 5 Life Lessons from Bonsai. Retrieved January 20, 2021, from https://bonsaiko.com/2016/06/26/5-life-lessons-from-bonsai/

Bonsaiko, T. (2017b, December 18). 5 Reasons BONSAI will benefit your HEALTH. Retrieved January 15, 2021, from https://bonsaiko.com/2015/01/05/bonsai-for-health/

Castillo, R. (2019a, November 27). 10 Best Reasons You Should Have a Bonsai Tree at Home. Retrieved January 15, 2021, from https://www.bonsaitreegardener.net/general/reasons-bonsai-tree-home

Castillo, R. (2019b, November 27). How To Use Fertilizer To Grow Your Bonsai Tree. Retrieved January 16, 2021, from https://www.bonsaitreegardener.net/care/feeding-fertilizer

Castillo, R. (2019c, November 27). Pine Bonsai Tree Care Guide. Retrieved January 15, 2021, from https://www.bonsaitreegardener.net/bonsai-trees/species/pine

Cicada. (n.d.). Retrieved January 18, 2021, from https://www.bonsaiforbeginners.com/cicada.html

Creating a Bonsai group planting : South Staffs Bonsai Society. (n.d.). Retrieved January 16, 2021, from http://www.southstaffsbonsai.co.uk/creating-a-bonsai-group-planting/

Deadwood bonsai techniques. (2020, December 13). Retrieved January 17, 2021, from https://en.wikipedia.org/wiki/Deadwood_bonsai_techniques

Deadwood on Bonsai. (n.d.). Retrieved January 17, 2021, from https://www.bonsaiempire.com/basics/styling/advanced/deadwood

Deciduous Bonsai | Basic Bonsai Tree Care. (2020, May 20). Retrieved January 15, 2021, from https://www.basic-bonsai-tree-care.com/deciduous-bonsai/

Difference Between. (2019, April 8). Difference Between Deciduous and Coniferous Trees. Retrieved January 15, 2021, from https://www.differencebetween.com/difference-between-deciduous-and-vs-coniferous-trees/

Dupuich, J. (2017, July 9). What to look for in surface roots. Retrieved January 17, 2021, from https://bonsaitonight.com/2016/08/09/what-to-look-for-in-surface-roots/

Dupuich, J. (2018, February 20). Signs that it's time to repot. Retrieved January 17, 2021, from https://bonsaitonight.com/2018/02/20/signs-time-repot/

Elliott, S. (2020, January 27). How Bonsai Works. Retrieved January 15, 2021, from https://home.howstuffworks.com/bonsai4.htm

expensive tools. (2013, November 27). Retrieved January 16, 2021, from https://www.bonsainut.com/threads/expensive-tools.13294/

FAQ. (n.d.). Retrieved January 20, 2021, from http://www.bonsaicarebasics.com/faq.html

Five Species That Make Great Indoor Bonsai. (2020, November 20). Retrieved January 15, 2021, from https://dengarden.com/gardening/Five-Species-That-Make-Great-Indoor-Bonsai

Google. (n.d.). Google Trends - Bonsai. Retrieved January 15, 2021, from https://trends.google.com/trends/explore?date=all&q=bonsai

Graham's Guide to Repotting Bonsai. (n.d.). Retrieved January 17, 2021, from https://www.kaizenbonsai.com/bonsai-tree-care-information/graham-s-guide-to-repotting-bonsai

Grow a Bonsai: The best guide to grow your own bonsai. (2018, August 29). Retrieved January 16, 2021, from http://growabonsai.com/

Harrington, H. (n.d.). Choosing the Right Pot for your Bonsai. Retrieved January 16, 2021, from http://bonsai4me.com/AdvTech/ATChoosing%20the%20Right%20Pot%20for%20your%20Bonsai.htm

Herons Bonsai. (n.d.-a). FAQs - How to Care for Bonsai | Your Bonsai Questions Answered | Herons Bonsai. Retrieved January 20, 2021, from https://www.herons.co.uk/Content/191/FAQs

Herons Bonsai. (n.d.-b). Forests & Group Bonsai Trees | Herons Bonsai Nursery. Retrieved January 16, 2021, from https://www.herons.co.uk/Outdoor-Bonsai/Forests-Groups-Bonsai/

Herons Bonsai. (n.d.-c). Herons Bonsai UK | Tree Seeds For Bonsai - Buy Now. Retrieved January 16, 2021, from https://www.herons.co.uk/Tree-Seeds-For-Bonsai/

Herons Bonsai. (n.d.-d). Outdoor Bonsai Trees | Herons Bonsai UK | Bonsai Tree. Retrieved January 15, 2021, from https://www.herons.co.uk/Outdoor-Bonsai/

How and When to Re-Pot Your Bonsai Tree | BonsaiOutlet.com. (n.d.). Retrieved January 17, 2021, from https://www.bonsaioutlet.com/how-and-when-to-repot-your-bonsai-tree/

How Much Light Does a Bonsai Tree Need? | Basic Bonsai Tree Care. (2020, May 21). Retrieved January 16, 2021, from https://www.basic-bonsai-tree-care.com/how-much-light-does-a-bonsai-tree-need/

How to Prune a Bonsai Tree. (2020, November 3). Retrieved January 17, 2021, from https://www.wikihow.life/Prune-a-Bonsai-Tree

How to Trim a Bonsai. (2020, October 4). Retrieved January 17, 2021, from https://www.wikihow.com/Trim-a-Bonsai

I think one of the biggest and most common mistakes with bonsai is trying to start from stock that is too young. What mistakes do you see often? (2012, July 17). Retrieved January 20, 2021, from https://www.reddit.com/r/Bonsai/comments/wppy9/i_think_one_of_the_biggest_and_most_common/

Identifying Common Bonsai Tree Insects and Pests | BonsaiOutlet.com. (n.d.). Retrieved January 18, 2021, from https://www.bonsaioutlet.com/common-bonsai-tree-insects-and-pests/

Insect Pests. (n.d.). Retrieved January 18, 2021, from https://www.bonsaiforbeginners.com/Insect_Pests.html

Johnson, L. (2017, November 9). 7 Oldest Bonsai Trees in the World. Retrieved January 15, 2021, from https://www.oldest.org/nature/bonsai-trees/

Just Fun Facts. (2020, June 21). Interesting facts about bonsai | Just Fun Facts. Retrieved January 15, 2021, from http://justfunfacts.com/interesting-facts-about-bonsai/

Khurana, P. (2017, June 13). Bonsai: Small Trees, Big Misconceptions | Matthaei Botanical Gardens and Nichols Arboretum. Retrieved January 20, 2021, from https://mbgna.umich.edu/bonsai-small-trees-big-misconceptions/

Kurtz, R. (2020, November 17). Care Instructions for the Adansonia Digitata Bonsai Tree. Retrieved January 18, 2021, from https://homeguides.sfgate.com/care-instructions-adansonia-digitata-bonsai-tree-75797.html

Larrimer, L. (n.d.). Why Join? | Membership. Retrieved January 20, 2021, from https://www.midwestbonsai.org/membership/why-join

Lieu, D. (2020, November 20). How to Repot a Bonsai Tree (and the Reasons for Doing So). Retrieved January 17, 2021, from https://dengarden.com/gardening/How-to-Repot-a-Bonsai-Tree-and-the-Reasons-Behind-It

List of species used in bonsai. (2020, December 2). Retrieved January 20, 2021, from https://en.wikipedia.org/wiki/List_of_species_used_in_bonsai

Loucks, J. (2020, September 21). How to Root Trim Bonsai Trees Before Cutting. Retrieved January 17, 2021, from https://homeguides.sfgate.com/root-trim-bonsai-trees-before-cutting-28072.html

Love for Bonsai. (2021, January 9). Is Bonsai Cruel? 6 Major Arguments Against Bonsai. Retrieved January 15, 2021, from https://loveforbonsai.com/is-bonsai-cruel/

Manion, J. (2020, April 8). How Often Do You Water A Bonsai Tree | Basic Bonsai Tree Care. Retrieved January 16, 2021, from https://www.basic-bonsai-tree-care.com/how-often-do-you-water-a-bonsai-tree/

mealybug. (n.d.). Retrieved January 18, 2021, from https://www.bonsaiforbeginners.com/mealybug.html

Meislik, J. (n.d.). Ten Greatest Bonsai Fallacies. Retrieved January 20, 2021, from https://www.bonsaihunk.us/Fallacies.html

Misconceptions And Truths About Bonsai. (2020, March 3). Retrieved January 20, 2021, from https://coloroutsidethelines.in/2020/02/27/misconceptions-and-truths-about-bonsai/

Mythbusting the Bonsai Tree: 13 Myths Unmasked. (2019, July 1). Retrieved January 20, 2021, from https://www.mythicalbonsai.com/mythbusting-the-bonsai-tree-13-myths-unmasked/

Mythical Bonsai. (2019a, July 1). 18 Amazing Facts About Bonsai Trees. Retrieved January 15, 2021, from https://www.mythicalbonsai.com/18-amazing-facts-about-bonsai-trees/

Mythical Bonsai. (2019b, July 1). Mythbusting the Bonsai Tree: 13 Myths Unmasked. Retrieved January 15, 2021, from https://www.mythicalbonsai.com/mythbusting-the-bonsai-tree-13-myths-unmasked/

Mythical Bonsai. (2019c, July 1). The Origin And Meaning of Bonsai. Retrieved January 13, 2021, from https://www.mythicalbonsai.com/the-origin-and-meaning-of-bonsai/

Nakamura, A. (2019a, November 27). How To Care For Outdoor Bonsai Trees. Retrieved January 16, 2021, from https://www.bonsaitreegardener.net/care/how-to/outdoor

Nakamura, A. (2019b, November 27). How to Display your Bonsai Using Stands. Retrieved January 20, 2021, from https://www.bonsaitreegardener.net/care/how-to/display-using-stands

Nakamura, A. (2019c, November 27). How To Get Rid Of Pests & Diseases For Your Bonsai Tree. Retrieved January 18, 2021, from https://www.bonsaitreegardener.net/care/how-to/pests-diseases

Nakamura, A. (2019d, November 27). How To Position Your Bonsai Tree. Retrieved January 20, 2021, from https://www.bonsaitreegardener.net/care/how-to/position

Nakamura, A. (2019e, November 27). How to Use a Stand/Table to Display your Bonsai Outdoors. Retrieved January 20, 2021, from https://www.bonsaitreegardener.net/care/how-to/stand-table-display-outdoors

Nakamura, A. (2019f, November 27). Types of Bonsai Trees. Retrieved January 20, 2021, from https://www.bonsaitreegardener.net/bonsai-trees/types/list

Nakamura, A. (2019g, November 27). What Does Bonsai Mean and Symbolize? Retrieved January 15, 2021, from https://www.bonsaitreegardener.net/general/symbolism

New England Bonsai Gardens. (n.d.). Retrieved January 20, 2021, from https://www.nebonsai.com/beginning/

Nickson, J. (2019, October 30). Are Bonsai Trees Poisonous To Dogs? Retrieved February 5, 2021, from https://growyourbonsai.com/are-bonsai-trees-poisonous-to-dogs/

P., R. (2020, September 12). Meaning and Symbolism of Common Bonsai Trees. Retrieved January 15, 2021, from https://florgeous.com/bonsai-tree-meaning/

Passion Vine Hopper. (n.d.). Retrieved January 18, 2021, from https://www.bonsaiforbeginners.com/passionvine_hopper.html

Preserving Bonsai Deadwood. (n.d.). Retrieved January 17, 2021, from https://www.kaizenbonsai.com/bonsai-tree-care-information/preserving-bonsai-deadwood

Problems With Your Bonsai? Top Seven Signs Of Trouble! (2016, April 13). Retrieved January 18, 2021, from https://www.bonsaioutlet.com/bonsai-articles/problems-with-your-bonsai-top-seven-signs-of-trouble/

Rhoades, H. (n.d.). Creating A Cascade Bonsai - Shaping and Style. Retrieved January 18, 2021, from https://www.gardeningknowhow.com/houseplants/bonsai/creating-a-cascade-bonsai.htm

Richards, K. (2020, September 3). What type of bonsai tree is best for you? Retrieved January 20, 2021, from https://www.bhg.com.au/bonsai-for-beginners

Scale Bonsai Insect Pests. (n.d.). Retrieved January 18, 2021, from https://www.bonsaiforbeginners.com/scale.html

Sears, C. (2020, October 27). 9 Popular Types of Bonsai Trees. Retrieved January 20, 2021, from https://www.thespruce.com/popular-types-of-bonsai-trees-5025687

Simson, W. (2019a, November 27). Coniferous Bonsai Trees. Retrieved January 15, 2021, from https://www.bonsaitreegardener.net/bonsai-trees/types/coniferous

Simson, W. (2019b, November 27). How To Air Layer Bonsai Trees. Retrieved January 17, 2021, from https://www.bonsaitreegardener.net/care/how-to/air-layering

Simson, W. (2019c, November 27). How to Display Bonsai Using Benches. Retrieved January 20, 2021, from https://www.bonsaitreegardener.net/care/how-to/display-benches

Simson, W. (2019d, November 27). How to Display your Bonsai Using Shelves. Retrieved January 20, 2021, from https://www.bonsaitreegardener.net/care/how-to/display-shelves

Simson, W. (2019e, November 27). How to Keep a Bonsai Tree Alive Indoors. Retrieved January 16, 2021, from https://www.bonsaitreegardener.net/care/how-to/alive-indoors

Simson, W. (2019f, November 27). How To Keep Bonsai Tree Leaves Small. Retrieved January 17, 2021, from https://www.bonsaitreegardener.net/care/how-to/small-leaves

Simson, W. (2019g, November 27). How To Protect Bonsai In Winter. Retrieved January 18, 2021, from https://www.bonsaitreegardener.net/care/how-to/protect-Winter

Simson, W. (2019h, November 27). The Practice Of Displaying Bonsai Trees. Retrieved January 20, 2021, from https://www.bonsaitreegardener.net/general/display

The 6 most common bonsai care mistakes. (2021, January 13). Retrieved January 18, 2021, from https://www.mistralbonsai.com/en/the-6-most-common-bonsai-care-mistakes/

The Basics of Bonsai Soil. (2018, June 15). Retrieved January 16, 2021, from https://www.basicbonsai.com/bonsai-soil/

The biggest mistake you wished you had avoided as a beginner. (2007, August 30). Retrieved January 20, 2021, from https://www.bonsainut.com/threads/the-biggest-mistake-you-wished-you-had-avoided-as-a-beginner.78/

The National Bonsai Society. (n.d.). Bonsai FAQ. Retrieved January 20, 2021, from http://thenationalbonsaisociety.co.uk/faq.html

The Why and When of Repotting your bonsai trees. (n.d.). Retrieved January 24, 2021, from https://www.bonsaitree.co.za/blogs/tree-talk/55461187-the-why-and-when-of-repotting-your-bonsai-trees

Toombs, I. (2014, March 14). Bonsai b*llocks – myths, lies and legends. Retrieved January 20, 2021, from https://brilliantbonsai.wordpress.com/2014/03/12/bonsai-bllocks-myths-lies-and-legends/

Top 5 Common Myths Related to Bonsai Plants & Its Gardening. (2019, August 12). Retrieved January 20, 2021, from https://www.blog.greendecor.in/top-5-common-myths-related-to-bonsai-plants-its-gardening/

Tovar, E. (2020a, May 23). Bonsai Fertilizer: Best Types and How to Use. Retrieved January 16, 2021, from https://florgeous.com/bonsai-fertilizer/

Tovar, E. (2020b, September 12). 64 Popular Types of Bonsai Trees You Can Grow. Retrieved January 20, 2021, from https://florgeous.com/types-of-bonsai-trees/

Westland. (2019, October 28). How to Choose a Bonsai Tree - Houseplant Advice - Westland. Retrieved January 15, 2021, from https://www.gardenhealth.com/advice/indoor-growing/how-to-choose-a-bonsai-tree

Why Do My Bonsai Keep Dying? | Basic Bonsai Tree Care. (2020, August 11). Retrieved January 18, 2021, from https://www.basic-bonsai-tree-care.com/why-do-my-bonsai-keep-dying/

Your Bonsai Will Thank You For Avoiding These Common Mistakes! (2015, May 11). Retrieved January 20, 2021, from https://www.bonsaioutlet.com/bonsai-articles/your-bonsai-will-thank-you-for-avoiding-these-common-mistakes/

Other Books in This Series

www.ingramcontent.com/pod-product-compliance
Lightning Source LLC
Chambersburg PA
CBHW030303100526
44590CB00012B/504